A KOREAN WAR ODYSSEY

BRINGING HOME UNCLE DONNIE
- MIA IN KOREA SINCE 1950

TOM GORMLEY

Print information available on the last page.

ISBN: 978-1-4907-9920-9 (sc)
ISBN: 978-1-4907-9919-3 (hc)
ISBN: 978-1-4907-9918-6 (e)

Library of Congress Control Number: 2020900347

Trafford rev. 01/17/2020

 www.trafford.com

North America & international
toll-free: 1 888 232 4444 (USA & Canada)
fax: 812 355 4082

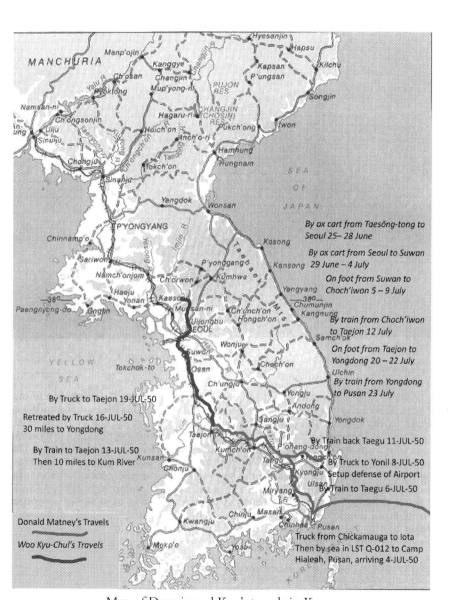

Map of Donnie and Kyu's travels in Korea

CONTENTS

ACKNOWLEDGMENTS

The picture of the young soldier with the ears sticking out graced my mother-in-law's kitchen forever. When asked, she would reply that her younger brother Donnie disappeared during the Korean War at the tender age of eighteen. In 2010, my wife, Sandy, and I set out to discover what happened to Corporal Donald Matney and to bring him home. Our journey took us to Washington, DC; Seoul, Korea; and many places in between. But slowly, carefully, step-by-step, we reconstructed the short life of Sandy's uncle Donnie, identified his remains, and returned him to rest by his mother's side in Missouri.

Along the way, we met many others who were involved in a similar quest. Among these were Pam Brekas, Tony Jasso, Carlos Corona, and the others whom we accompanied to Korea in 2017 with the help of Sunny Lee and Mike Badzioch of the Revisit Korea Program. Of course, we could not have located Uncle Donnie without the research of John Zimmerlee. William "Shorty" Cox was also instrumental to our journey, guiding us through the intricacies of the US Army Personnel Recovery Program. Thanks to all who welcomed Uncle Donnie home to his third and final resting place, including the Missouri Patriot Guard, Missouri Highway Patrol and all of the fire departments along the way. And a special thanks to Glenn Perkins, Jerry Abendroth, Ted Ringer, Angela Drake and Clay Bonnyman Evans for their insights, edits, and encouragements.

Though Sandy's mom and her aunt Anna never knew what happened to Uncle Donnie, it was their perseverance that led Sandy and I to take up the quest. Aunt Ruth participated as best she could and knew that Donnie was buried by their mother prior to her passing, and Donnie's youngest sibling, Uncle Leonard, who keeps soldiering for the Lord, was there when Donnie was laid to rest.

This book is dedicated to them and to all who are still looking for their loved ones lost in the Forgotten War.

INTRODUCTION

Pam Brekas, niece of MIA Cpl. Wayne B. Gill Jr.

Not knowing—not knowing what really became of your son, your father, or your uncle—is the worst. What happened to him while serving in Korea? Was he subject to the torture of being a Prisoner of War (POW)? How long did he really survive, and where and how did he die? Will we ever know any of this?

To family of missing service personnel, these questions linger forever in the recesses of their minds. As spouses, siblings, and other relatives of the missing pass away, another generation may take up the call to find our loved ones who went missing almost seventy years ago.

It is vital that our government do whatever they can to find their remains and repatriate them. With new DNA techniques, closure comes to many but not all. Thousands of families still do not know what happened.

Sadly, my ninety-six-year-old mother went to the grave not knowing what happened to her brother, only wanting the family to ultimately be together. This uncle of mine knew me and loved me when I was a baby. I only got to know him as I read his letters that always asked about me.

For those who have these lingering questions, we implore our nation to go forward in the search for answers. With the DPAA and the Coalition of Families working on finding answers, we also need the positive reinforcement, support, and funding from our government to get final resolution.

This book gives answers for only one of the missing. It is a start. See the struggle to get answers and find resolution.

INTRODUCTION

John Zimmerlee, son of MIA Cpt. John H. Zimmerlee Jr.

World War II ended. The United States took the lead in reestablishing peace and guided Japan in returning control to the countries they had overtaken. But when they approached the Korean predicament, North Korea had become communist and under the influence of China and Russia. Thus, returning South Korea to North Korea posed problems. The logical solution was to encourage South Korea to be a free nation, and we spent five years preparing them for independence. We failed. As soon as we pulled out, China invaded, and we had no choice other than supporting South Korea in battle. The Korean War started, and soldiers like Donald Matney were immediately sent into harm's way and were lost in battle.

Three years later, the war ended but in a ceasefire, not a victory. The losses were overwhelming. Families of the still missing were told not to discuss the war and to suffer their losses quietly.

Meanwhile, hundreds of remains were recovered from the battlefields. Many were preliminarily identified, but due to the lack of dental background information, they were just buried as unknown and the families were never consulted.

For sixty years, the forensic files of these unidentified warriors remained classified until our government accidentally released them along with those of World War II. It was then when dedicated family members like Sandy and Tom Gormley took the lead and demanded current scientific technology to be applied.

It takes passion, persistence, and dedication to get our government to admit their errors. Writing a novel like this one is far beyond our expectations. All Americans, young and old, need to read this story. It is a time in history that resembles our current situation, and we all should be familiar with the past in order to make better decisions in the future!

DAYBREAK, **25 JUNE 1950**, TAESŎNG-TONG, KOREA

The rooster crowed and warned the evil spirits of the night that it was time to leave, but the thunder-like roars still rumbled in the background, ignoring their cry. Kyu yawned, stretched, and carefully got out of bed to begin his chores, not wanting to wake his wife and daughter. Korea may be known as the Land of the Morning Calm, but this day wasn't starting that way. He heard more rumblings in the distance, and there were numerous lightning-like flashes in the dawn's early glow. Outside, the earth was wet, so it had rained during the night, and the storm remained still growling in the distance. Kyu left the house, fed the goats and chickens, and hitched the oxen to the yoke to start another day on the farm. His wife and daughter would be up soon to make breakfast. His mom always slept late on Sundays, so she would not be stirring yet. His stomach growled at the thought of Nabi's warm cooking. The thunder-like rumble grew, accompanied by a mechanical rattling noise sounding somewhat like a train. No normal storm made noises like that.

As Kyu walked from the barn, the foot-tall *ssal julgi* (rice stalks) in the *non* (rice fields) waved gently in the water, fertilized by human and animal dung. Woo Kyu-Chul and his ancestors have raised rice on this farm outside of Taesŏng-tong for centuries. His grandfather was here when the Japanese *jjokbari* invaded in 1910 and built the Gyeongwon railroad. It ran from Seoul, the new capital in the south, through Kaesŏng, the old capital west of here, to Wonsan in the north. Maybe the mechanical sound was a new type of train? Kyu didn't know, and it didn't seem to be threatening, so he continued with his chores.

During his grandfather's day, the Japanese *wae-nom* did not tolerate disrespect and would harshly discipline at the least infraction. His grandfather did not like the *wae-nom,* and they tortured and killed him as an example. His grandmother survived somehow and raised their only child, his father, under the Japanese watchful eye until he turned fourteen. Then the *wae-nom* took him away to be educated. He returned three years later and soon married a local girl. Kyu was born not long after in 1932. When Kyu turned ten, his dad was taken again to enlist in the Japanese army. That was because he refused to change his Korean name to Japanese. Kyu has been the head of the Woo household ever since. He never saw or heard from his father again.

After that, Kyu's *Eomma* (mom) raised Kyu by herself. Using her meager earnings, she hired help to keep the farm productive and teach Kyu traditional Korean values and ethics under the Japanese watchful eyes. The *wae-nom* required everything in school be taught in Japanese, but *Eomma* made sure the farmhands taught Kyu Korean history and culture. They even taught him Hangul, the Korean alphabet, which was illegal. The farmhands also taught him how to defend himself the Korean way using tae kwon do. Even under Japanese occupation and high taxation, they survived. Certainly there were times during the occupation when they had to mix barley with the rice to make a meal because the Japanese took the rice. There was even a short period when they had to eat chicken feed *gijang* (millet). But they always had enough to get by. Then the Japanese were defeated in 1945, and things became better.

When Kyu turned fifteen, *Eomma* knew he would need help on the farm. Kyu's interests turned to more than just animals and farming. It was time to find Kyu an *anae* (wife). *Eomma* worked within the Woo clan and picked out a suitable bride for Kyu from Kaesŏng before he turned sixteen. When he met her, Kyu thought Nabi was the most beautiful butterfly that he had ever met. He fell madly in love with her.

A year later, the *seon* (arranged wedding) occurred at the house of Nabi's parents at dusk. Grim-faced and hiding his emotions, Kyu rode to the house on a borrowed horse while his *girukabi* (wedding leader) and groomsmen walked. When they arrived, he presented Nabi's mother with a *kireogi* (wild goose) and bowed twice in respect. Geese mate for life, so Kyu was promising a long life of love and care for Nabi. It was a traditional *kunbere* (wedding ceremony) with both Kyu and Nabi wearing gilded *hanbok* dresses. A *samulnori* percussion quartet played before the ceremony, and Nabi's sisters performed a *buchaechum* (fan dance). Kyu was seventeen and Nabi sixteen when they were married as calculated by the traditional Korean method for determining age. They sealed their vows by bowing and sipping wine in a gourd that Nabi's mother provided. After the wedding, Nabi moved in with Kyu on the family farm. Through their love, their daughter Sa-rang was born, with the traditional blue Mongolian birthmark on the small of her back. Kyu thought he would work the farm in peace with Nabi and Sa-rang forever now that the Japanese were gone.

The end of the war in 1945 split Korea in two, with the Russians accepting the Japanese surrender north of the 38th parallel and the United States accepting it south. Taesŏng-tong straddled the line between the two countries but fell under control of the south. Kyu didn't much care. He paid his taxes and worked the farm—raising two oxen, a couple of goats, and some chickens with Nabi and their young daughter Sa-rang—and left politics to others. They had relatives in the South who claimed Syngman Rhee, president of the Republic of Korea (ROK), would make them all rich and that Premier Kim Il-Sung from the North, or the Democratic People's Republic of Korea (DPRK), would take everything away. His cousins in the North said just the opposite. Kyu didn't believe either side. He was just glad that the Japanese were defeated and he could raise his family in peace on the centuries-old farm. Sure, there were stories that the North wanted to reunite Korea by force and rule the entire peninsula, but Rhee also claimed he was the rightful president of all of Korea. He had heard the stories that the ROK Army fought off several North Korean attacks. Many were killed—they said maybe as high as ten thousand died in these skirmishes during the past year—but Kyu didn't know anyone who had perished and the closest episode had happened over by Kaesŏng in May last year. These events seemed to be happening more frequently along the border to the east but not around Taesŏng-tong.

Kim Il Sung   Syngman Rhee

Unknown to Kyu, Kim Il-Sung aspired to reunite the Korean peninsula by force. Issuing a manifesto on 8 June 1950, Kim proclaimed elections be held throughout Korea early in August for seats in a new parliament to meet in Seoul on 15 August, the fifth anniversary of the liberation from the Japanese. This parliament would establish a government for a united Korea with Kim elected as premier. With the help of the Soviets, he planned to ensure this destiny by massively invading the South. He expected an immense popular revolt to simultaneously arise across the South to spread the quick collapse of the ROK government. So under the pretext of holding military training maneuvers, he deployed 90,000 soldiers (with another 45,000 in reserve) supported by 150 Soviet tanks near the 38th parallel. And on Sunday, 25 June at 4:00 a.m., just when Kyu was getting up, they opened fire and started advancing south along the entire peninsula. Unbeknownst to Kyu, his small village of Taesŏng-tong would straddle the divide between ideologies for the next sixty-plus years.

★ ★ ★

The North Korean People's Army (NKPA, or *Inmun Gun*) was well prepared by the Soviets. Up to fifteen Soviet advisers were embedded within each infantry division to provide training and guidance. Their equipment, though not always new, was a mixture of Soviet and Chinese products and was well maintained. Their large howitzers could shell far in advance of their infantry. The NKPA even controlled a small air force of forty fighters, seventy attack bombers, sixty YAK trainers, and ten reconnaissance planes. Thousands of spies and saboteurs infiltrated the South to wreak havoc and destroy key installations in advance of the army attack. Many of the NKPA troops were veterans of the Chinese Revolution of 1949 and war with the Japanese. They had seen many atrocities and would soon participate in more of their own.

The Republic of Korea (ROK) Army, though they did not realize it, was woefully ill prepared to meet this onslaught. Abandoned by the Allies after Rhee's election, only a handful of American military advisers and observers helped the South Koreans. The American government feared arming South Korea as they felt Rhee might choose to invade the North. Hence, the ROK equipment was a hodgepodge of World War II leftovers from both the Americans and the Japanese armies. They had no tanks and only light artillery. Their air force consisted of ten advanced AT-6 trainers and twelve liaison-type planes. Of the sixty-four thousand soldiers in the ROK Army that Sunday morning, only thirty-four thousand, considered the best, faced North Korea. The rest were scattered throughout the South, training in small unit tactics and chasing guerrillas.

★ ★ ★

Just then, three trucks filled with armed soldiers, menacing in appearance, bounded up the road in front of Kyu's farm and headed north. As Kyu watched them pass, he noticed billowing clouds of smoke in the distance in the dawn's brightening glow. The lightning he saw earlier was coming from those clouds. The sounds must be explosions and not thunder. It must be another North Korean rice raid, but this incursion from the North was bigger and closer than the others. Though rattled, Kyu still had to check the *jebang* (levees) around his rice paddies before breakfast to make sure that the rodents hadn't breached them and lowered the water. Otherwise, his rice would die.

DAYBREAK, **25 JUNE 1950**, CAMP CHICKAMAUGA, BEPPU, KYUSHU, JAPAN

or Donnie Matney, Sunday mornings in the army were the best. Unless deployed on maneuvers, Sundays were always relaxed. Sure, he still had to get up for reveille, but here in occupied Japan, army life was different. Since the dropping of the atom bombs and the total dismantling of the Japanese military economy, the Japanese people had nothing, and the US government (and thus, the army) didn't worry about Japan and Asia. The world powers believed the Soviet Union was now the enemy, and they would soon attack West Germany and take over Europe. Japan was beaten. China wasn't a threat. Europe was much more important to protect than any country in Asia. So the Nineteenth Regiment of the Twenty-Fourth Infantry Division performing occupation duties in Japan received few supplies and new equipment from the States. They had to improvise, and the easiest way to improvise to everyone's benefit was to employ the Japanese civilians to do things. By January 1950, when Donnie arrived, the army employed the Japanese to do just about everything—cooking, cleaning, gardening, and even guard duty was performed by the Japanese on base.

Donnie couldn't believe army life at Camp Chickamauga. Being fresh from boot camp at Fort Riley, Kansas, and only passing through Fort Lawton in Seattle, Washington, Japan was his first real posting.

The many days spent on the troopship traveling from Seattle to Japan were horrible. Most of the soldiers in transit spent the entire trip hugging the rails, seasick. Everyone on board thought that they would be assigned a tough billet in the real army upon arrival in Japan. They expected to end up working their butts off—more so than during their eight weeks of basic training. That thinking could not have been more misguided. When Donnie finally arrived on 4 January 1950, he reported to base and was assigned to Howe Company to become part of a four-man 81 mm mortar squad. When he checked in with Sergeant First Class Joseph Szito that Wednesday, the sergeant told him to go find a bunk, settle in, and meet at the mess hall at 1800. So he walked into the barracks expecting it to be empty in the middle of a Wednesday afternoon. Instead, he found most of the bunks full of snoozing GIs. When he asked what was going on, he was told "Welcome to the life of a Chick." As the Japanese did everything, there wasn't much to do most afternoons, except sleep, write letters, and listen to the armed forces radio station.

Donnie soon learned the glorious history of the Nineteenth Regiment. Formed in 1861, the Nineteenth was known as the Rock of Chickamauga due to the strength and courage of its enlisted men who successfully defended their position during the Civil War battle at the West Chickamauga[1] Creek in Georgia. For over three days in September 1863, 65,000 Confederates battled 60,000 Union soldiers resulting in over 34,600 combined casualties. Near the battle's end, a lowly second lieutenant assumed command of the remains of the Nineteenth Regiment when the other officers were killed or wounded. Under his command, they held their position at Horseshoe Ridge, providing enough time for the rest of the Union Army to form new defensive positions in Chattanooga thus earning them their moniker. The regiment later fought valiantly in the Indian Wars, World War I, and in World War II, where they were deployed from Hawaii and Australia to help liberate the Philippines.

Colonel Guy S. Meloy Jr. commanded the Nineteenth Regiment in Japan in 1950. Along with the Twenty-First and Thirty-Fourth Regiments, the Nineteenth Regiment was part of the Twenty-Fourth Infantry Division, the Victory Division, symbolized by a taro leaf insignia worn on every soldier's shoulder. The Twenty-Fourth

---

1 *Chickamauga* roughly translates to "river of death" from its native Cherokee language.

Infantry Division was commanded by Major General William F. Dean. General Dean reported to Lieutenant General Walton H. Walker, Eighth Army Commander, who in turn reported to General Douglas MacArthur, commander in chief of the Far East Command. Howe Company morning reports that Sunday in June listed 120 GIs assigned with 115 on active duty. Though companies were typically led by a captain, Howe Company was commanded by First Lieutenant Paul F. Reagan. Sergeant First Class (SFC) Joseph S. Szito commanded the mortar platoon and was Donnie's direct superior noncommissioned officer. Donnie was pleased to learn that General Dean served as a captain in the Nineteenth Infantry fourteen years previously and that the general always took an interest in the activities of the Chicks.

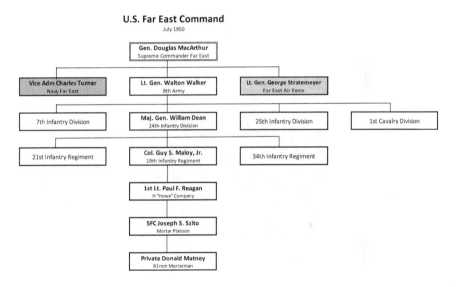

U.S. Far East Command
July 1950

This late June Sunday, Donnie planned to go to church services at the base chapel and then go fishing. That is, unless one of his buddies could hook him up. Then he would either go roller skating, dancing, or to the movies to entertain a local girl. Most of the privates first class and servicemen with higher ranks had a "moose." In Japan at this time, families were so poor that they could not afford to feed their children once they became teenagers, so certain arrangements were made. The boys got apprenticeships or jobs in the base and the girls set up apartments with the GIs footing the bill. The servicemen then shacked up with the *musime* (girl) and attended other events with them when they could get off base. And with no regular duties, getting permission to stay off base was easy. But Donnie's pay as a buck private wasn't enough to make ends meet and support a "moose." Besides, Donnie had heard the lectures from the chaplain about the evils of sex with the natives and had seen the VD slideshows. So Donnie just entertained when one of his troop mates needed a friend for a friend.

★ ★ ★

Donnie was born Donald Eugene Matney on 11 April 1932 in Matney Hollow near Seymour, Missouri. He was the eighth of nine children born to Willa McKinley Tarbutton and Silas Floyd Matney. His dad delivered mail to help make money to support the farm. His dad was also a bit of a daredevil and owned an early motorcycle. Unluckily, he died when Donnie was six, and Willa had to move off the farm into the town of Seymour to get a job to support the three youngest children who were still living at home. Donnie didn't remember much about his dad. His older brothers were the ones who taught him the ropes, including how to hunt and fish.

Silas Matney on motorcycle

Growing up in Missouri was mostly fun for a young boy intermixed with work. There were woods to explore and trees to climb and streams to go fishing and skinny-dipping in (if you didn't mind the leeches). Mostly Donnie liked to hang out with his friends. Seymour, Missouri, was a small farm town of less than one thousand located east of Springfield and known for growing apples. It was a whistle-stop on the Frisco train line and had one stoplight. Starting in 1932, the year Donnie was born, Route 60 jogged through it, bringing a gas station and diner to town. But not much else existed, except the apple orchards and the Carnation milk company. Donnie never traveled much as a kid, but he did go with his mom to visit his big sister and her family in Colby, Kansas, once when he was fourteen. Of course, while they were there, he got a toothache and had to have a tooth extracted. It was just his luck. His one big adventure outside of Seymour and he loses a tooth! They did drive past Fort Riley on the way to Colby, and he saw all the army troops and equipment. That was when he first got the itch to join the army.

It seemed like someone in the Matney family was always in the military. Donnie's great-great-great-grandfather fought in the Revolutionary War with Nathanael Greene in the Carolinas. After the war, he was rewarded with a section of land along the Pee Dee River. He settled there but, after a while, got the itch to explore. So he traded his land in the Carolinas for land in the Missouri territory. That's how Matney Hollow came to be.

Donnie Matney Sophomore in 1949

During the Civil War, Donnie's great-grandfathers Elijah Matney, James Tarbutton, and Wiley Copley fought for the North in the Webster County Missouri militia while his great-grandfather M. Bryant Ipock, living in Tennessee, may have fought for the South. His dad was in the army for a while but was too old for World War I. His older brother Billy was a tanker in Germany during World War II. Billy had lots of tales of the things he did and saw. Donnie and his good friend Chuck Farr often talked and dreamed about joining the army and getting out of Seymour to see the world. Finally, Chuck said he was going to do it. So Chuck and Donnie went to meet with the recruiter. Chuck was a year older, and he signed up right away. Donnie's mom had to approve his papers. He was only seventeen at the time and had just completed his sophomore year of high school. She agreed because she knew Donnie had the Matney wanderlust and she would no longer have to feed a hungry teenage boy. Besides, what risk was there in peacetime in the army? A younger classmate, sixteen-year-old Joe Peters[2], drove Donnie and Chuck Farr to the train station on 17 August 1949 for their journey to boot camp at Fort Riley. Little did they know that it would be the last time all three friends would be together.

The eight weeks spent at Fort Riley in basic training passed quickly. Having spent most of his youth outside, Donnie was in good shape and didn't have any problems with calisthenics. He also did well at the range as he had a rifle at home and hunted to help supply meat for the family. They also poked and prodded him, examined his teeth, gave him shots, and took chest X-rays to check for tuberculosis. When he first arrived, he was a wiry 120 pounds on a five-foot, eight-inch body. The drill sergeants called him lots of names during basic training, mostly deriding his red hair and rail-thin frame. When he left, he was a solid 132 pounds. The drill sergeants also stopped yelling derisive nicknames and started calling all the soldiers GIs.[3] Donnie

---

2   Joe Peters lived a full life in Seymour, Missouri, had a shotgun wedding, got divorced, then married his high school sweetheart. He died after he learned that Donnie had been found. He was buried the same day in the same cemetery where Donnie was reinterred.

3   *GI* originally came from the words *galvanized iron* that were stamped on the metal equipment used by the Cavalry in the late 1800s. By World War II, it was adapted to mean "government issue" as all soldiers completed the same basic training.

didn't see much of Chuck during basic, but they both made the trip from Fort Riley to Fort Lawton and then on to Japan. Donnie was assigned to the Nineteenth Infantry Regiment. Chuck got hitched to the First Cavalry Division as an armored reconnaissance crewman. They tried to stay in touch, but it was difficult as they were stationed on different Japanese islands. First Cavalry was deployed to Honsho around Tokyo while the Nineteenth was deployed south on the island of Kyoshu. Donnie planned to visit Chuck and see Tokyo the next time he got a three-day pass. They said that the girls there were prettier and more sophisticated than the ones near Camp Chickamauga and were always willing to entertain a man in uniform.

Donnie's time at Camp Chickamauga seemed more like an extension of high school than service in the military. With the Japanese performing most of the mundane tasks at camp, the regiment established all kinds of sports teams just to keep the boys busy and active. General MacArthur was quoted saying, "Upon the fields of friendly strife are sown the seeds that, upon other fields, on other days, will bear the fruits of victory."[4] Football, baseball, basketball, boxing, bowling, horseshoes, table tennis, softball, golf, volleyball, and swimming were all organized into team sports that the Chicks could participate in. Each team competed against other regimental teams within the Twenty-Fourth Infantry Division. The best players for each sport from each regiment then formed the Big Green Team within the Twenty-Fourth Infantry Division to compete in the All-Japan Championships against the other Eighth Army Divisions.

The army was still an army, and training to fight did occur. The Nineteenth Regiment attended the deliberate defense, attack, and counterattack training sessions in January and March 1950 at the Shimamatsu training area, but that was the only real army training that Donnie attended. He did go to the shooting range every week or so to fire a rifle. He stripped and cleaned his rifle after every time on the range just like he did at home. Not everyone did that. Though everyone in the infantry was to be proficient with a rifle, in Japan, they were not required to shoot and were not taught how to disassemble a rifle and clean it. His squad also practiced with the M1 81 mm mortar. Donnie could hump the forty-five-pound baseplate and help set it up in just over a minute, but they never fired any live

---

4   *The Organization Day Yearbook of the Nineteenth United States Infantry Regiment*, September 20, 1949

rounds while in Japan. There just didn't seem to be any reason. They did launch a couple of M301 illumination rounds one night over the Camp Chickamauga parade grounds as a lark. They were quite bright, and Sergeant Szito ripped the squad leader a new one when they got caught. Donnie's squad became as proficient practicing with the mortar as could be expected without ever firing a single live round.

★ ★ ★

The church service in the chapel this June Sunday morning was sparsely attended. Most of the regiment skipped out or spent the night with their moose. God wasn't a priority to soldiers living the good life during peace on occupational duty. Though a Baptist by creed, Donnie liked the nondenominational service preached by the chaplain.

After the service, he went back to the mess hall to get lunch. He was still careful eating as he had his wisdom teeth removed a while back there in Japan and his gums were still tender. While in line, someone said that the armed forces radio had something on it about North Korea declaring war on South Korea. Supposedly, the premier of North Korea, Kim Il-Sung, claimed that South Korea had rejected every North Korean proposal for peaceful unification and had attacked North Korea that morning near Haeju above the Ongjin Peninsula. North Korea retaliated in self-defense and had begun a "righteous invasion." Syngman Rhee,[5] president of South Korea, was to be arrested and executed. Of course, only a few of the old-timers really knew where North and South Korea were located as the Twenty-Fourth Infantry had been posted there briefly after the war. Most didn't realize that Korea was less than six hundred miles to the west, just across the Sea of Japan.

Donnie ate lunch but skipped desert. He now weighed 142 pounds, the most that he had ever weighed. None of Donnie's buddies needed a friend for company that afternoon, so Donnie went fishing. He caught three nice chub mackerels, which were a new type of fish to him as they didn't grow in Missouri. He let them go.

---

5   Syngman Rhee was also derisively called Rhee-Shung-Man by the North
     Koreans.

```
    ... ...
ARB19
AX23
RR UAP ZVA
RR UAPC JAPHQ UAPh.. UHPB UEPSE 555

DE UAPOH 18
R 260149Z
FM FBIS OKINAWA
TO UAPC/CINCFE TO' ) JAPAN
INFO JAPHQ/CG FEA} TOKYO JAPAN
UAPKA/USIS SEOUL KOREA
UHPB/INTELINFOCEN FTSHAFTER TH
UEPSE/FBID WASHDC
                FBID GRNC

B260149 PYONGYANG IN KOREAN TO KOREA SUNDAY JUNE 25 1950 1300 GMT--B
  (COMMENTARY IN DIALOGUE FORM--EXPOSITION OF THE CRIMES OF
SYNGMAN RHEE)
  (SINGLE EXCERPT)
  MAN--THAT IS NOT RPT NOT ALL. FINDING HIMSELF AT THE END OF HIS
WITS IN OBSTRUCTING THE PEACEFUL UNIFICATION OF THE FATHERLAND,
SYNGMAN RHEE HAS AT LAST EMBARKED ON THE SOCALLED NORTHERN EXPEDITION
WHICH HE HAS SO GLIBLY BEEN TALKING ABOUT.
  WOMAN--YES, IT IS REPORTED THAT THE GANG, THAT IS THE SOCALLED
NATIONAL DEFENSE ARMY, LAUNCHED EARLY THIS MORNING ARMED INVASIONS
AGAINST AREAS NORTH OF THE THIRTYEIGHTH PARALLEL ALONG ITS ENTIRE
LENGTH.
  MAN--YES. UNDER ORDERS OF BANDIT SYNGMAN RHEE THE GANG STARTED
A CIVIL WAR. THEREFORE, THE PEOPLE'S ARMY OF THE REPBLIC AND THE
GUARD CORPS OF THE MINISTRY OF HOME AFFAIRS RESOLUTELY FOUGHT BACK
AND BEGAN A RIGHTEOUS INVASION. THEREFORE, BEFORE LONG THE OLD
BANDIT SYNGMAN RHEE WILL BURN TO DEATH IN THE FLAMES OF THE CIVIL
WAR IGNITED BY HIMSELF.
  WOMAN--SO IT IS NONE OTHER THAN SYNGMAN RHEE HIMSELF WHO IS
RESPONSIBLE FOR THE FATHERLAND STILL REMAINING DIVIDED.
  MAN--OF COURSE, HIS BASTARD IS THE TOP CRIMINAL WHO HAS BEEN
BSTRUCTING THE UNIFICATION AND INDEPENDENCE OF OUR FATHERLAND.
THEREFORE IT IS NO ACCIDENT THAT HIS NAME SHOULD HAVE BEEN AT THE
TOP OF THE LIST OF CRIMINALS WHOSE ARREST HAS BEEN PROPOSED.
  WOMAN--INDEED. HE IS THE MOST SINISTER TRAITOR OF TRAITORS.
  MAN--THEREFORE, THIS KIND OF BAYOARD MUST NEVER BE TOLERATED.
HE MUST BE ARRESTED AND EXECUTED FORTHWITH.
  WOMAN--QUITE. HE SHOULD NEVER BE LEFT AT LARGE. SUCH MEN SHOULD
BE ROUNDED UP AND EXECUTED EN MASSE.
  MAN--ANYWAY, THE KOREAN PEOPLE ABSOLUTELY DEMAND THAT THIS
SINISTER ENEMY BE ARRESTED. THE KOREAN PEOPLE CAN NO LONGER
TOLERATE THEM. IN PARTICULAR, FATHERS, MOTHERS AND CHILDREN
OF THE LARGE NUMBER OF THE PATRIOTS WHOM THIS BASTARD HAS MASSACRED
ARE ANXIOUSLY LOOKING FORWARD TO THE DAY WHEN HE IS ARRESTED AND
EXECUTED. THIS BASTARD MUST RECEIVE PEOPLE'S EXECUTION. THAT DAY
IS NOT RPT NOT FAR OFF. 251330 MILLER
                          26/0158Z JUNE
```

Translation of NK War Radio Announcement

MIDAFTERNOON,
25 JUNE 1950,
TAESŎNG-TONG, KOREA

Kyu completed inspecting his rice paddies. All the *jebang* surrounding each *non* were in good shape with no leaks and at least eight inches of water in them. He did bag a couple of slow *jwi* (rats) with his *kal* (knife) while making his rounds. He hoped Nabi would include them into tonight's *bosintang* (dog soup) for meat as he hadn't caught any stray dogs. *Bosintang* (dog soup) was traditionally eaten during the hottest days of the year to enhance male stamina. Kyu hadn't had any this year, and he hoped his wife would make some tonight. He really wanted another baby—a son to take over the farm. With the smoke and the explosions continuing in the north and now appearing in the east and west, Kyu thought he might need more stamina but not for the traditional reasons. Too bad he couldn't catch any wild dogs.

Just then, another group of army trucks sped up the road headed north. They had the markings of the Thirteenth Regiment of the ROK First Division on them. The soldiers in them looked grim. Kyu had heard that the Thirteenth Regiment was deployed around Korangp'o-ri to the east. They were supposed to be the best regiment in the ROK. This incursion had been going on for hours now with no sign of abating. In fact, if anything, based on the smoke clouds and noise now in every direction but south, it appeared to be intensifying. Hopefully the Thirteenth could force the North back soon. Unbeknownst to Kyu, the North Koreans had already captured his wife's hometown of Kaesŏng, causing little damage to that historic city. They were now marching south along the whole peninsula.

★ ★ ★

The Korean peninsula is shaped like Florida but with the

panhandle facing east instead of west. Situated in the eastern part of Asia, it is connected to China to the north and Russia to the northeast at the tip of the panhandle. Japan is located 600 miles to the east across the Sea of Japan. The Yellow Sea separates it from the rest of China and Taiwan to the west. It varies from 90 to 200 miles in width and from 500 to 625 miles in length. It is a hilly peninsula where only 20 percent of the land is arable and the rest is quite mountainous, hitting heights of 8,500 feet above sea level. In a land mass the size of Utah, 30 million people called it home in 1950—21 million in the South and 9 million in the North. It is hot and humid during the summer when the monsoons come and can be quite frigid in the winter when the winds blow in from Mongolia.

On this Sunday, it was quite hot with occasional monsoonal showers. The 38th parallel was chosen as an arbitrary division between the countries during the Potsdam Conference near the widest section of the peninsula without regard to natural features. When it was divided, most of the natural resources, industry, and electrical output lay in the North while most of the people and agriculture lay in the South. Taesŏng-tong, where Kyu lived, had rolling hills rising from the valley of the Imjin River and was located right at the 38th parallel.

Kyu wondered if his neighbor had heard anything about what was happening. Though no one in Taesŏng-tong had electricity or running water for that matter, his neighbor seemed to always know the latest news and gossip. So Kyu walked down the road to see what he could learn. When he got there, he was surprised to see his neighbor frantically piling belongings into his wagon. He told him that he had heard from the soldiers that North Korea had declared war and was invading the South. Kaesŏng had already been captured. It was not just another rice raid. The latest soldiers to pass through were with the reserve Eleventh Regiment trying to reinforce the Thirteenth. The Thirteenth Regiment was holding Korangp'o-ri but would soon have to fall back below the Imjin River in order to make a stand. He insisted that we all needed to cross the Imjin before they retreated or we would be in the murderous hands of the North.

Kyu ran back to his farm and quickly attached his two yoked oxen to his simple two-wheeled *kateu* (farm cart). He then ran into his house and yelled at Nabi to pack quickly. She looked at him quizzically, and he rapidly filled her in on what their neighbor had told him. Having heard the explosions and seen them extending all around, she wasted no time packing. He knew that she and Sa-rang would not be safe if the North caught them here at the farm. She was too young and pretty. Who knew what they would do to her, their daughter, and his *eomma* (mom)? They had to make it across the Imjin River and then to Seoul and finally across the Han River before the communists came to really be safe.

25–28 JUNE 1950, CAMP CHICKAMAUGA, BEPPU, KYUSHU, JAPAN

Stories and rumors flew during the afternoon and evening in the barracks. Armed Forces Radio claimed that armed bandits from the North were invading South Korea. Kimpo Airport had been strafed, wounding an American private who was part of the Korean Military Advisory Group (KMAG), the US Army personnel who remained in Korea to train and observe the ROK. A feeling of uneasiness settled over the barracks that evening. The bunks were full as all leaves were summarily canceled. The moose would be lonely from then on.

The next morning after reveille, the company marched to the parade ground from their barracks, and Donnie was surprised to see the other companies of the Nineteenth in tight formation as well. Though nothing official had come down through the ranks, a certain tension buzzed in the air. After breakfast, Lieutenant Reagan tasked a squad to go over to the armory and draw out live ammunition. They were shocked to discover everything covered in rust. The machine gun ammunition metal belts were so rusted that they were immovable and useless. That Monday, those assigned to guard duty were Americans instead of Japanese, and they carried live ammunition for the first time. That really got Donnie's attention.

The lieutenant also started rearranging assignments and establishing a new heavy machine gun squad and another heavy mortar squad. He also handed out promotions, but Donnie didn't get one, at least not yet. Additional personnel were transferred into the company from other Eighth Army divisions in Japan, bringing the total assigned to Howe Company on the books to 136. Though no orders had been cut, preparations were being made.

The five-year-old United Nations met overnight and demanded the North Koreans cease hostilities and withdraw back to the 38th parallel. President Truman authorized ships and airplanes to protect the mandatory evacuation of American dependents from Korea. He also authorized the use of armed air and naval forces as needed to support the ROK below the 38th parallel.

By 28 June, US planes were attacking targets of opportunity in Korea. Flying from Japan, eight fighters using rockets and .50-caliber machine guns strafed a convoy of NKPA trucks and tanks two miles south of Munson. Six trucks, apparently loaded with gasoline, were left in flames and three tanks destroyed. The same fighters also claimed to have strafed marshaling yards, a small depot, and a concentration of six to seven hundred troops six miles south of Munson. Six additional tanks were also attacked and two were left burning. Six B-26 bombers attacked the airfield at Onjin and damaged the runway. This early in the conflict, no antiaircraft fire or interceptors were noted. However, one B-26 and one F-82 made emergency landings at Suwon due to damage sustained from ground fire. While there, three NK Yak-9 planes strafed the airport and destroyed the two planes.

Though the Nineteenth Infantry Regiment had yet to be called to duty, others were already entering the fray. Morale remained high, but so did confusion. During the last week of June, the company drilled in camp in earnest. The previous preparedness evaluation in April assessed the Twenty-Fourth Infantry Division at 65 percent in combat readiness, the lowest ranking of any infantry division in the Eighth Army. They had plenty of room to improve and maybe not much time to do it. Live rifle fire was held daily. Obstacle courses were run. Calisthenics were performed. Though Donnie's squad worked with the mortar, they still did not fire any live rounds. That would have to wait for another time.

25–28 JUNE 1950,
NORTH OF SEOUL, KOREA

The road was crowded with other farmers and refugees fleeing Taesŏng-tong and vicinity from the oncoming battle. Kyu and his small family made it to the bridge at Korangp'o-ri at dusk. The ROK still protected it. They crossed the Imjin River and stayed in the outskirts south of town, resting for almost six hours. Among their belongings and food, Nabi brought kimchi (fermented cabbage), rice, and dried fruit for a late dinner. It didn't look like Kyu would be getting *bosintang* (dog soup) for quite a while. The next morning, they started south on the highway with the others toward Seoul, expecting it to take at least two days to walk the forty-plus miles with the oxen in tow. Kyu walked the whole time, guiding the oxen and keeping them steady, when an army vehicle sped by. Kyu's wife, mother, and daughter rode in the cart. Nabi kept surprising Kyu with small treats. How she was able to do it when they only had an hour to pack and leave the farm he would never know, but he was certainly glad and very appreciative.

Due to the short notice, only the bare necessities were loaded into the cart. They had a seat for Kyu's *eomma*, who had been silent the whole time. The baby was still breastfed so she did not require much. Besides the oxen, Nabi had put a couple of chickens into a cage and tied a nanny goat to the cart. Potable water was brought in wrapped clay jars and should not be a problem while traveling as it could be replenished from the monsoonal rain. They had two changes of clothes each. Rice and barley and some other grains were loaded for the oxen and chickens, and the oxen could also graze. Nabi kept pulling out additional food, including at least two types of kimchi. She had even packed a paper packet of *gotgam*, his favorite sweet of dried persimmons. Kyu of course brought the small sum of emergency money that they kept and his *kal* (knife) for protection.

The ROK First Division and Thirteenth Regiment held Korangp'o-ri and the Imjin River position for three days against the superior NKPA forces. They finally withdrew when it became clear that they were being flanked and would be cut off. They retreated to the southwest. Unluckily, the NKPA was so close behind that the orders to destroy the Imjin bridge could not be completed. The bridge fell intact to the North. The ROK First Division headed to the Han River. On the way, it was strafed by US fighter planes on 28 June. Colonel Paik Sun-Yup, in charge of the division, commented to his officers after the strafing, "You did not think the Americans would help us. Now you know better."[6]

Gen. Paik Sun-Yup

Kyu and his family made good time traveling until midafternoon on Monday. Then suddenly out of nowhere, an airplane flew out of the sun and strafed four ROK Army vehicles that were passing by the

6   Appleman, *South to the Naktong, North to the Yalu*, 24.

refugees. The vehicles exploded, and many of the soldiers were killed and wounded. Kyu tried to help, but they shooed him away. So the family plodded on for a couple of hours more. They stopped about eighteen miles short of Seoul on Monday evening.

On Tuesday, they awoke at sunrise and started walking on toward Seoul. The road was much more congested, and their speed slowed to a crawl. The baby started acting up, so Kyu's wife walked beside the cart with him for a while so that they both could entertain her. *Eomma* still rode in silence. The day was hot, but the afternoon monsoon cooled them and allowed them to top off their fresh water supply. They reached the outskirts of Seoul just after 1800.

The city was in chaos! The fear was palpable as all thought the North Koreans were just a few miles away. Nabi wanted to stay the night some place, but Kyu told her they must cross the Han River tonight if possible. So they kept walking and joined the throng on the main thoroughfare leading through town to the Hangang Bridge. Jammed with all types of vehicles and pedestrians, eight lanes of traffic moved at a snail's pace south toward the bridge. Slowly they progressed. Finally, they could see the bridge, and it, too, was overloaded with traffic of all types. They kept plodding along and reached the double spans of the highway bridge at 2:00 a.m. Kyu was exhausted, and everyone else was asleep in the cart. He was surprised that the oxen could even move. Barely making any headway, they started across the bridge. They were within sight of the south side when suddenly there was a gigantic explosion! The center two spans of the bridge that they had just crossed blew up and dropped into the water still full of people and vehicles.

The assistant minister of defense for the ROK panicked. The last two ROK divisions protecting Seoul were lost, and the NKPA must be near. He ordered all the bridges across the Han River demolished *immediately*. He didn't care if they were full of people. He didn't care if most of the army and its heavy equipment had yet to cross. He needed to save the country by keeping the NKPA north of the Han. His order was carried out, and the majority of the ROK's military vehicles were stranded on the wrong side of the river. Over five hundred people perished in the collapse of the main auto bridge that Kyu and his family had just barely crossed. The NKPA were not near and did not make it to the center of Seoul for another twelve hours. It was a disaster.

The shock of battling tanks for the first time without any effective counter weapons was the largest contributing factor to the fall of Seoul within the first four days of the war. Colonel Paik Sun-Yup and the fighting First Division forged the Han near Kimpo on 29 June with just over 5,000 soldiers of their original 9,715. With no bridge to cross, their armament consisted of what they could carry. The rest of their equipment and artillery was left on the northern side of the Han River for the NKPA to exploit. Of the 98,000 active soldiers and police in the ROK on 25 June, only 54,000 were combat-ready at the beginning of July. Over 45 percent of its soldiers were gone and just 30 percent of its heavy weaponry remained after the first few days of battle. They needed help and supplies desperately.

25–30 JUNE 1950,
ELSEWHERE

In an emergency session across the international dateline on 25 June, the United Nations Security Council met in its temporary facility[7] at Sperry Corporation's headquarters in Lake Success, New York, to condemn the actions of North Korea. They passed a resolution that North Korea's actions "constitutes a breach of the peace" and called for (1) an immediate cessation of hostilities, (2) North Korea to withdraw their armed forces north of the 38th parallel, and (3) all UN members to provide South Korea assistance and refrain from assisting North Korea.[8] Voting for the resolution was China (Taiwan),[9] Cuba, Ecuador, Egypt, France, India, Norway, United Kingdom, and the US. Yugoslavia abstained, and Russia was absent (protesting the seating of the Republic of China in the UN).

President Harry S. Truman was vacationing at his family home in Independence, Missouri, when he learned about the North Korean invasion. At the urging of Secretary of State Dean Acheson, he flew back on the presidential C-118 Liftmaster, dubbed Independence, to Washington, DC, that day. While the White House was being

---

7   Groundbreaking ceremony for the UN building in New York City at Turtle Bay occurred on 14 September 1948 and was declared complete on 10 October 1952.

8   UN Security Council Resolution 82 was passed on 25 June 1950.

9   The People's Republic of China (mainland) would not be seated in the UN until 1971 under President Nixon.

renovated, President Truman and the Joint Chiefs of Staff met at Blair House to discuss the Korean situation. Using the instantaneous long-distance communications method of the day, the teletype, they conferenced with General MacArthur, supreme commander of Far East, while he was in Japan. They authorized him to provide ammunition and equipment to Korea, to provide ships and planes to safely evacuate Americans, and to send a survey party to Korea to evaluate the situation and report back. Truman also ordered the Seventh Fleet to leave the Philippines for Japan and to report to MacArthur. Based on the KMAG reports, MacArthur reported that he felt Korea would not survive without immediate support. Truman and the Joint Chiefs conferenced again with MacArthur via teletype on 26 June and authorized him to use naval and airpower against all North Korean military forces south of the 38th parallel.

Harry S. Truman

The United Nations Security Council passed a second resolution on 27 June requesting member nations to give military aid to South Korea to help repel the North's attack. The resolution ended with "[recommendations] that the members of the United Nations furnish such assistance to the Republic of Korea as may be necessary to repel the armed attack and to restore international peace and security in the area."[10]

---

10   UN Security Council Resolution 83 was passed on 27 June 1950.

The situation in Korea meanwhile was chaotic. All KMAG personnel were ordered to evacuate along with all other US nationals. Unluckily, many were north of the Han River when the bridges were blown and were thus cut off. Finally, using threats of force, most KMAG personnel were ferried across the Han late on the morning of 28 June, including the acting US commander who was traveling with the secure, encrypted radio truck. They trekked to Suwon and met the Korean command and Brigadier General John H. Church whom MacArthur had sent as his aid to evaluate the situation and take command of US forces. That evening, using the secure radio, General Church advised General MacArthur that the US would need to commit ground troops to restore the original boundary. MacArthur decided to evaluate the situation himself and flew into Suwon the morning of 29 June.

General MacArthur insisted upon driving the twenty-two miles from Suwon to the Han River. Along the way, there were thousands of refugees and disorganized ROK soldiers fleeing the battle area. He reached the Han and observed the NKPA forces across it on the northern side. He informed General Church that he agreed the situation required the immediate commitment of ground forces and he would request such authorization from Washington that evening. He left Suwon by 17:15 for Japan.

Back in Japan, MacArthur provided his on-site assessment that ground troops would be necessary to stop the invasion via another teletype conference with the Joint Chiefs. By midmorning on 30 June, President Truman approved flying a regiment to the combat zone immediately, sending two divisions to Korea from Japan by sea and establishing a naval blockade of North Korea. Truman decided to call the hostilities in Korea a police action, which allowed him to deploy troops without the approval of Congress and a declaration of war. However, he ordered MacArthur that under no circumstances were the Americans to engage in any direct hostilities with either the Russians or the Chinese or near their borders with North Korea. In response, General MacArthur ordered General Walton H. Walker, Eighth Army commander, to send two infantry divisions to Japan at once. General Walker in turn issued Comnav Order 7-50, sending the Twenty-Fourth Infantry Division to Pusan via naval ship command with Far East Air Force (FEAF) providing support and cover. The Twenty-Fourth Division was chosen as the first division to be deployed solely because it was the closest to Korea even though it was assessed as the least combat-ready of any division in the Eighth Army.

With that momentous decision, America was committed to ground battle on the Korean peninsula, and though he didn't know it yet, Donnie Matney was going to war.

29 JUNE–4 JULY 1950,
BEPPU, KYUSHU, JAPAN

Donnie couldn t believe the change in the attitudes and actions of Howe Company within a week. All were confident that they could stop the bandit North Koreans in this police action within a couple of days. The NKPA would see the vaunted US Infantry that had conquered the Germans and the Japanese during the last war, and they would flee in terror back to the north. Though they trained rigorously during this short time, Donnie could tell that the months of inactivity had really hurt his stamina and conditioning. The extra pounds didn't help much either. They still hadn't fired any live rounds through the mortar.

The new guys transferring in were from other divisions within Japan and weren't in any better physical shape. They, too, had been pampered by the Japanese doing everything. But they, too, thought this would be a simple romp across the Sea of Japan and then back to visiting with the moose. Most of the soldiers were in their early twenties. Donnie was among the youngest at eighteen. Only a few served during World War II, and most of them had never seen combat. The 10 percent who had been in combat previously were more nervous than the rest.

General Dean of the Twenty-Fourth Division directed Lieutenant Colonel Charles "Brad" Smith to assemble a delaying force of two rifle companies, two heavy mortar platoons, and a platoon of 75 mm recoilless rifles from the Twenty-First Infantry Regiment to fly to

Pusan, Korea. His orders were to "advance at once to the North by all possible means, contact enemy now advancing south from Seoul toward Suwon and delay his advance."[11] Colonel Smith had been at Schofield Barracks, Oahu, Hawaii, on that fateful December 7 when the Japanese attacked Pearl Harbor. There he took D Company, Thirty-Fifth Infantry to Barbers Point and commanded the first US Army shots fired in anger during World War II. Now he was being tasked to do the same against another enemy who had led a surprise attack, the North Koreans.

Only six C-54 transport planes were available to take Task Force Smith from the airfield at Itazuke, Japan, to Pusan, Korea, on that rainy Saturday morning. General Dean was there in Itazuke to greet Colonel Smith. Using a map from National Geographic as an aid, General Dean told him to stop the North Koreans as far north of Pusan as possible. The first plane took off at 0845 on 1 July, and Colonel Smith quickly followed in the second. The rest of the planes were airborne within hours. Unluckily, when they arrived in Korea, Pusan was fogged in, so the first two planes turned around and flew back to Japan without landing. Colonel Smith would not land in Korea until the tenth flight.

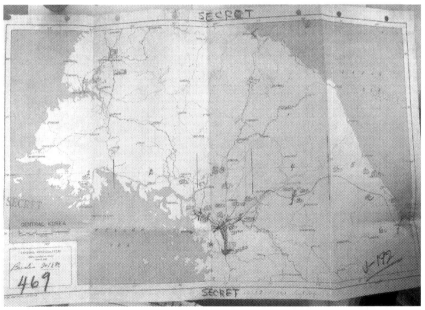

Intelligence Map of NKPA Invasion

When they all finally arrived in Pusan, a ragtag group of 150 trucks and vehicles rounded up by KMAG drove them to the train station seventeen miles away by 1500. The road was crowded with well-wishers waving flags, banners, streamers, and posters. A few NKPA spies were sprinkled among them, checking their weaponry and taking a headcount. A Korean band played at the rail station completing the circus-like atmosphere. The train left by 2000 headed north. Unluckily, only half of the heavy mortars and recoilless rifles were put on board. The rest sat in boxes and pallets at the rail station in Pusan—not that they would have made any difference to the final outcome.

The train with Task Force Smith arrived at Taejon in the middle of South Korea by 0800 on 2 July. Colonel Smith met with General Church, who told him that he only needed a few men who won't run at the sight of tanks to give the ROK moral support. Colonel Smith replied that he would go north and look over the terrain to locate an appropriate location to make a stand. Smith and his officers then set off north on an eighty-mile journey over bad, bumpy roads toward Osan. They saw thousands of ROK soldiers and refugees along the road streaming south. Three miles beyond Osan, Colonel Smith located a ridge about three hundred feet above the road and railroad with a clear view of Suwon eight miles to the north. He issued orders to make this their defensive position for a stand. The rest of the task force traveled by train from Taejon to P'yongt'aek, fifteen miles south of Osan, and bivouacked there on 3 July. Six 105 mm howitzers from A Battery, Fifty-Second Field Artillery Battalion, joined the task force with 108 men. The first US battle with the North Koreans was set to be held at a knoll just north of Osan.

General Dean ordered the Twenty-Fourth Infantry Division to head to Korea. The remainder of the Twenty-First Infantry Regiment sailed to Pusan first to join with Task Force Smith. The Thirty-Fourth Infantry Regiment followed a day or so behind. Donnie's Nineteenth Infantry was told to pack unnecessary items for storage and prepare two days of personal items. Donnie hurriedly wrote a letter home to his mother, Willa, telling her that he was headed to Korea and may not be writing for some time. Among his personal items, he included fishing hooks, a skate key, two small copies of the New Testament, and a Bible. As this was to be a police action, he thought there should be downtime to have fun fishing and maybe roller skating while in

Korea. He thought Korea might have different fish than at home and the chub mackerels he had caught near Camp Chickamauga in Japan. The company was issued 120 live rounds of rifle ammunition each on 2 July and told to have their packs ready by 1300. A long line of one-and-a-half-ton trucks pulled into Camp Chickamauga around that time. Donnie saw Camp Chickamauga for the last time at 1800 on 2 July. They drove for forty-five minutes to the port in Oita, Kyusu, and there the 131 soldiers of Howe Company boarded the LST (landing ship, tank) Q012 bound for Pusan, Korea.

Lieutenant Reagan noted that the weather was fair but morale very good in the morning report during that two-day journey across the Sea of Japan. During the voyage, Donnie and most of the men thought that they were going to die at sea before ever stepping on land in Korea. The flat-bottomed LST was heavily loaded and pitched and rolled quite violently in that fair weather. Almost everyone was seasick. To make matters worse, the lieutenant had the heavy machine gun crews mount their weapons on the corners of the LST just in case the North Korean air force attacked. Now whoever heard of a bunch of criminals having an air force? What type of a police action were they really entering?

Howe Company arrived in Pusan, Korea, at 1900 on 4 July 1950 and marched five miles with their equipment to Camp Hialeah to bivouac for the night. There were no enemy shots or fireworks for that matter to greet them. As they were among the last of the Twenty-Fourth Division's companies to arrive in Korea, Camp Hialeah at least had latrines and defensive positions already dug. They only had to pitch their two-man tents, eat warm grub for the first time in two days, post guards, and go to sleep to recuperate from their harrowing sea voyage. And then they would begin their part of the police action. Some of the troops wondered when they would get their deputy badges. Again, the weather was noted as fair and morale as very good by Lieutenant Reagan in the morning report.

29 JUNE–4 JULY 1950,
SOUTH OF SEOUL, KOREA

As a farmer, Kyu was used to getting by on just a few hours of sleep, but Nabi and little Sa-rang were not. The stress of traveling as refugees was already taking a toll on them. His *eomma* was still silent. They rested fitfully just south of the destroyed bridge across the Han from Seoul. The next morning, their fellow refugees suggested they go to Suwon and board a train south to Taejon or even Taegu. Kyu thought traveling further south sounded like a good idea but didn't think that it would be possible to get his oxen and cart onto a train. They would just keep walking.

Kyu and his family were lucky to get across the Han River Bridge when they did. Deploying the Seventh and Second Divisions, the ROK mounted a counterattack against the NKPA just north of Seoul. It turned into a rout. The NKPA tanks and heavy artillery devastated the lightly armed ROK infantry. The crack NKPA Third and Fourth Divisions marched into Seoul and gathered fleeing ROK soldiers, police, and national traitors, whom they summarily shot. They established People's Committees from South Korean communists already there to run the city. They dispersed the majority of the older population out of the city as refugees to cause strife and confusion, and they pressed anyone between the ages of fifteen and thirty-six into service in the NKPA with the goal of raising 450,000 conscripts. Had they stayed the night in Seoul, Kyu would have either been shot or become an unwilling NKPA soldier.

Instead, they plodded south through the industrial city of Yongdungp'o with a large crowd of refugees. There were occasional bursts of artillery fire from the North Koreans across the Han that landed nearby and scared both the animals and the refugees, but mostly it was just drudgery trudging south along with thousands of others. They still had food, but the grain for the oxen was getting low. They needed to get into the countryside so that the oxen could graze. Though this would slow them, there didn't seem to be any other alternatives. There weren't any *nongmin sijang* (farmer's markets) that Kyu could buy additional grain from for the oxen with his meager savings. Luckily, that evening, they made it to the south side of Yongdungp'o and found a field where the oxen could graze to stretch their scanty supply of grain.

Kyu normally slept under the cart while Nabi, Sa-rang, and *Eomma* slept inside. The long days of walking helped Kyu to sleep like a rock, but that night, a noise roused Kyu around 0300. Though there were many other refugees in the field with Kyu, three *dodug* (thieves) in what looked like tattered army uniforms were rummaging through the back of the cart. Kyu grabbed his *kal* (knife) that he always kept nearby and yelled menacingly at them. They just laughed and kept looking through Kyu's meager possessions, taking what they wanted and discarding the rest. Of course, they took the packet of *gotgam*, his favorite sweet of dried persimmons. One pulled a pistol, called Kyu a *deoleoun nongbu* (dirty farm boy), and told him to back off. Kyu was humiliated, but there wasn't much he could do. There were three of them with a gun and just him with a *kal* (knife). Those refugees around him who had awakened and whom he could see just looked down. Luckily, the *dodug* did not disturb his wife, child, or *Eomma*, who all had the good sense to stay still and not provoke them. After they left, Kyu leaned against the cart and sobbed quietly.

The next morning, Nabi put on a good front and told Kyu that the *dodug* had not taken anything of value—just a few minor items and a little bit of food. They would be all right, she insisted. No one was hurt. *Eomma* didn't say anything, so Kyu yoked the oxen, and they started on the road south toward Suwon. They made it to Anyang-ni, halfway between Yongdungp'o and Suwon, that evening. They made Suwon on the evening of 3 July.

★ ★ ★

After consolidating and rearming, the North Koreans began advancing out of Seoul. The NKPA Sixth Division crossed the Han River north of Seoul, captured Kimpo airfield, and marched on to Inchon. The crack NKPA Third and Fourth Divisions meanwhile crossed the Han and waged a bitter two-day battle with the ROK for Yongdungp'o. The ROK held their ground as the NKPA were unable to get any tanks across the Han until they repaired the main railway bridge. They completed the repairs on 3 July. Yongdungp'o fell around midmorning that day when the tanks entered the suburb. But the NKPA paid a heavy price as the Fourth Division lost 227 men and almost 2,000 were wounded or missing. By the morning of 4 July, two of the NKPA's best divisions were ready to resume driving south along the main rail highway axis toward Taejon. They felt that they were unstoppable. The ROK knew that they were.

4–5 JULY 1950, OSAN, KOREA

Meanwhile at P yongt aek, Colonel Smith mounted his task force for the fifteen-mile drive to the position staked out north of Osan and south of Suwon. The Korean truck drivers suddenly disappeared when they discovered that the Americans were headed north, so Colonel Smith ordered the GIs to drive the trucks. As they crossed one stream, they noticed Korean engineers wiring the bridge for demolition. They vainly tried to tell them that they needed the bridge for when they returned, but the Koreans continued wiring. Finally, the GIs grabbed the box of dynamite and threw it into the river below. The ROK engineers shook their heads in disbelief and left. It took the main part of the task force over two and a half hours to drive the fifteen miles to the defensive position as the road was crowded with refugees and ROK elements fleeing south. All the units in Task Force Smith made it there by early morning before sunrise. Colonel Smith had them dig foxholes and defensive positions along the ridge, and they were still making these preparations at dawn on 5 July. They parked their jeeps and vehicles south of the saddle with the artillery hidden behind the hill for supporting fire. To communicate, telephone wire was strung along the ground from Colonel Smith's command post at the top of the hill across the road to the artillery beyond. The artillery was armed with 1,200 high explosive rounds but only carried six of the eighteen anti-tank rounds that were currently available in all the Far East command. No anti-tank mines were allocated to the US in Asia. Army command felt they were all needed in Europe.

NKPA T-34 Tank & Crew

Though it was rainy, visibility was good, so Colonel Smith could see the first NKPA vehicles leaving Suwon by 0700. At 0816, he ordered the artillery to fire high explosive rounds at the first eight tanks. It was ineffective, and the tanks rolled on. They came into range of the recoilless rifles, but their shells also bounced off the sides of the tanks. Then bazookas were used, but these, too, did no damage, even to the less-protected rear of the tanks. Two of the tanks were finally stopped when the forward howitzer used the six anti-tank rounds. They pulled off the side of the road, and the rest of the tanks proceeded south after picking up the crewmen from the damaged tanks. Nothing Task Force Smith had could stop the tanks, except the expended anti-tank rounds. Additional tanks plodded by in groups of four, firing at the US infantry but not stopping. By 0900, twenty-nine of thirty-three tanks passed through Task Force Smith and continued their deadly march headed south. As they passed, the tanks also chewed through the telephone wire strung across the road connecting the artillery with Colonel Smith, thus isolating them from receiving commands and firing corrections.

About an hour later, Colonel Smith saw a long line of vehicles and infantry leaving Suwon with additional tanks interspersed. He estimated that this column was at least six miles long. When they closed within about one thousand yards, in his own words, he "threw the book at them[12]". Unluckily, with the rain, air cover was unavailable and planes could not be radioed in. Otherwise, the NKPA would have been decimated. For over an hour, tiny Task Force Smith fired on the two top NKPA divisions. As the tanks had chewed up telephone wiring, artillery fire was ineffective and the shells missed the NKPA convoy entirely. Soon the NKPA began a movement that they would perfect and perform numerous times in the future—the envelopment. While their gunfire held attention to the front, NKPA infantry swept to the left and right and attempted to roll up the US forces from the sides. Sensing this was happening, Colonel Smith ordered withdrawal at 1430, abandoning all crew-served weapons—recoilless rifles, mortars, and machine guns. The men were essentially left to escape on their own. Stationed behind the protection of the hills, most of the artillery crew was able to evacuate using their trucks. Colonel Smith joined with them, gathering about one hundred infantrymen along the way, but the remaining GIs had to walk back to friendly lines. One group ran into an NKPA machine gun nest that caused numerous injuries. The regimental baseball team captain, a lieutenant, grabbed a grenade and threw it over forty yards into the machine gun nest, destroying it. This was one of the few redeeming acts resulting from those lazy days of playing baseball and other sports while on occupational duty in Japan.

The dead and many of the wounded had to be left in place. A medical sergeant volunteered to stay with the thirty worst litter cases. They all disappeared, either taken prisoner or killed on the spot. At that time, the NKPA was ordered to take no prisoners, but they were surprised to be fighting Americans and took a number as prisoners of war (POW) at the urgings of the embedded Soviets. The Soviets felt that the captured Americans would be effective propaganda tools. The remaining walking wounded walked out. Though there was no real pursuit, it took many days and even weeks for some to make it back to friendly lines. General Church had told Colonel Smith that the ROK needed soldiers who could stand up to tanks. Unluckily, Task Force Smith could not.

---

12   Appleman, *South to the Naktong, North to the Yalu*, 73.

4–5 JULY 1950,
AROUND OSAN, KOREA

The airplanes came out of the south and strafed the entire road. Kyu and his family made it through Suwon early 4 July and walked toward Osan. While in Suwon, they purchased more kimchi, using about a third of their meager cash reserve and trading all their remaining chickens. *Eomma* was silent the entire time but did eat some kimchi. The oxen grazed along the road as they had finished the remaining grain. This slowed them down further. The Suwon rumor mill said that the North Koreans would arrive that afternoon. They hurried as quickly as grazing oxen would allow and were about a mile or so out of town when the airplanes struck. Kyu's wife and baby were walking along beside the cart, and Kyu was able to push them out of the way of the incoming bullets. The oxen and *Eomma* were not so lucky. *Eomma* went peacefully, having not uttered a single full sentence since they had left the farm at Taesŏng-tong. Kyu and Nabi, stricken with grief, hastily scraped out a shallow grave beside the road while hundreds of other refugees passed silently by. They buried *Eomma* and took what they could carry from the cart in makeshift *peuleim paeg*, (A-frame packs) made from the demolished cart. They left the ruined cart and dead animals by the side of the road and trudged on south with the rest of the refugees.

Sa-rang, not understanding why Nabi was crying, also started to cry. There was little that Kyu could do for either. He knew that they were now just barely ahead of the North Koreans. They had to keep walking. So he took his wife's bundle of possessions as well as his own and pulled her up with the baby. He cushioned her as best he could against his side and started walking as fast as he could. Still sobbing quietly, she followed along. They were down to a small amount of kimchi and rice, some water, his *kal* (knife), a change of clothes each, and the small amount of savings he salvaged and split among them.

Even though the war was only less than two weeks old, the UN forces ruled the skies, and the NKPA and its tanks already feared airplanes more than anything else. By the second week of the war, planes from the air force, navy, marines, and Australia were flying hundreds of sorties a day. Unluckily, they were just now getting coordinated support as forward controllers were moved to the airport in Taejon. Still, many mistakes were made, including the strafing of friendly ROK troops and refugees.

Kyu and Nabi kept walking with the other refugees. It seemed that they would never be safe again. There were still other men intermixed with the refugees that appeared to be ROK deserters, but Kyu couldn't be sure. Maybe they were actually North Korean infiltrators. He didn't see anyone who looked like the three *dodug* that had robbed them earlier. As they neared Osan, they could see a number of vehicles with tall pale men in strange uniforms standing by them, pointing this way and that. At this section of the road, the railroad made a wide curve to the east while the highway went over a rise before going into the valley where Osan was located. They could hear the tall men speaking in a foreign language. Kyu and Nabi continued on the road and made it to Osan about 1700. They were able to negotiate for rice from one of the few people still in town. The *ma-eul salam* (villager) who lived there told Kyu that the strange men and vehicles were Americans and that there were many more of them south at P'yongt'aek. He heard that they planned to fight the North Koreans where Kyu had first seen them.

Kyu, afraid of getting stuck in a battle, convinced his wife to keep walking. They had traveled many miles since the oxcart had been destroyed that morning, but Kyu wanted to go further. So they kept walking with the other refugees past dusk. Just then, a large number of those strange vehicles and trucks with Americans in them drove up from the south. The road was very narrow, and most of the refugees would not get out of the way, but the vehicles slowly passed. Some were pulling large cannons.

Kyu, Nabi, Sa-rang, and most of the other refugees walked for another hour or so before stopping a couple of miles south of Osan. The North Koreans were gaining on them. Hopefully, the Americans could stop or, at least, slow them.

6–8 JULY 1950, CH'ONAN AND SOUTH KOREA

General Dean, commander of the Twenty-Fourth Infantry Division, faced many problems. His regiments were poorly trained, out of shape, had questionable World War II–surplus weapons, none of which could stop a T-34 tank, and were spread out between Korea and Japan. General Walker, head of the Eighth Army, needed General Dean and the Twenty-Fourth Infantry Division to delay the superior NKPA forces long enough so that the rest of the Eighth Army could establish the defensive positions that would become known as the Pusan Perimeter. General Dean knew that if he could hold the NKPA between the Asan Bay at P'yongt'aek and the mountains near Ansong, they would be great targets for the air force. Once south of that line, the peninsula would widen, the NKPA would have room to spread out, and they would be harder to stop. The next obstacle on the west coast side of Korea would be the Kum River before Taejon. At this time, he had no real intelligence telling him how strong the NKPA really was. He was about to find out.

★ ★ ★

The First Battalion of the sister Thirty-Fourth Infantry Regiment arrived by train at P'yongt'aek the morning of 5 July while

47

Task Force Smith was battling the two NKPA divisions north near Osan. They deployed two companies about two miles north of town that evening and south of a small culvert whose bridge they destroyed at about 0300 on 6 July. They dug slit trenches, but most of these had six to eight inches of water at the bottom due to the monsoons and high-water table. The sound of running motors at 0700 caught the soldiers out of their foxholes eating K rations for breakfast. The noise was the lead elements of the NKPA Fourth Division infantry, including at least eighteen tanks. The tanks stopped at the blown bridge, but the infantry marched right through the small stream.

The First Battalion fired machine guns and mortars at the NKPA and may have destroyed a truck, but the NKPA infantry just kept coming. The infantry squad leaders opened fire with their rifles. About half of the men complained that their rifles would not work. After-action reports confirmed that these were either assembled wrong, had not been properly cleaned, or were damaged. They had not been checked by the troops before being deployed. The ones that could not be repaired were dropped into a well. The First Battalion commander was spooked and started a disorderly retreat south toward Ch'onan. In his candid post-action report, he stated, "Early overconfidence changed suddenly to surprise, then to dismay, and finally to the grim realization that, of the two armies, the North Korean force was superior in size, equipment, training, and fighting ability."[13] The withdrawal was chaos, and clothing and equipment littered the road as they retreated. They established a new defensive position just south of Ch'onan.

By then, three companies from the Twenty-First Regiment that had not been part of Task Force Smith and traveled by sea from Japan to Pusan made it by train to Ch'onan along with the Third Battalion of the Thirty-Fourth Infantry Regiment. They joined the defensive position just south of Ch'onan but sent a large contingent of the Third Battalion north to meet the enemy the morning of 7 July. As most of the batteries for the radios were old and failed quickly, communications between the companies and command were ineffective. The North Koreans also had jammed radio communications. The men of the Thirty-Fourth were ill-trained and afraid. Each was issued eighty to one hundred bullets, about enough

---

13   Hickey, *The Korean War: The West Confronts Communism*, 2001.

for ten minutes of fighting, and no hand grenades. When a small advanced party ambushed their commander in midafternoon, the majority retreated in haste and left him lying there wounded. Mortars, jeeps, and other equipment were left where they were lying, and the troops bugged out. The commander was captured and spent the next thirty-eight months as a prisoner of war. When no NKPA followed them, a small patrol from the Thirty-Fourth sheepishly went back and retrieved the mortars and jeeps that they had left behind. New positions were hastily made at the train station at the north edge of Ch'onan the evening of 7 July. They thought that the buildings and the quickly assembled defensive positions would protect them from the NKPA.

The NKPA had other ideas. Though the road was mined with antipersonnel mines, five or six tanks came into Ch'onan from the west (instead of the north) in the wee hours of the morning. They shot everything that could safely house an American—the train station, the church, several buildings, and every vehicle in sight. In this melee, the Third Battalion tried everything to stop the tanks. Two were taken out with grenades and bazookas. Private Leotis E. Heater threw five grenades onto one tank and set it on fire, but the rest of the tanks created havoc. The Third Battalion's commander was killed when a tank cannon shot physically cut him in half. The artillery stationed south of town was called in to provide a phosphorus smoke screen and, under its cover, only 175 of the Third Battalion made it back to the lines of the First Battalion arranged south of town. The NKPA claimed that they had taken over sixty prisoners from the battle of Ch'onan. Clearly the Thirty-Fourth's Third Battalion could not withstand the tanks either.

General Dean's fear of the NKPA breaking free of the choke hold between P'yongt'aek and Ansong was being realized. South of Ch'onan, the main road split with one part following the railroad southeast to Choch'iwon and the other running due south to the Kum River at Kongju. The roads converged back together with the rail line at Taejon. General Dean again split his meager forces, ordering the Thirty-Fourth Regiment to perform delaying actions along the western route and then set up defensive positions south of the Kum River at Kongju. He ordered the Twenty-First Regiment to follow the eastern route and establish another delaying action near Choch'iwon. His order to both groups on 8 June was this: "Hold the Kum River line at all cost. Maximum, repeat maximum delay will be effected."[14] He added to the Twenty-First that they must hold at Choch'iwon and cover the ROK left flank until the latter could fall back. No additional reserves would be available for four days. The fate of Taejon would be decided by the stand taken at the Kum River.

---

14   Appleman, *South to the Naktong, North to the Yalu, 90.*

6–9 JULY 1950, CHOCH'IWON, KOREA

Somehow, Kyu, Nabi, and Sa-rang made the thirty-mile journey from Osan to Choch'iwon on foot. Once, a group of motorcycles and a funny-looking small car with a gun turret on top passed them coming from the north. Kyu surmised that they were North Korean reconnaissance trying to discover the American and ROK positions. Luckily, they did not stop. Another time they saw a number of refugees milling about in the road ahead. Kyu wondered what was going on but finally determined that the North Koreans had set up a *lodeu beullog* (roadblock). These were not regular NKPA soldiers but appeared to be some other group. They were armed with rifles and had machine guns set up on both sides of the road. They funneled all the refugees through a line and went through everything that they were carrying. They took away most of the belongings and a lot of individuals, separating the young men from the older men and older women from the younger women.

He heard a number of gunshots but couldn't see who was shooting. As the North Koreans didn't seem excited, he figured that they must be doing it. There seemed to be a number of ROK deserters among the refugees, so Kyu thought that maybe they were executing them. Very few refugees were allowed past this *lodeu beullog* (roadblock), and the separated older men and women were given shovels and pitchforks and stood in a group off to the side guarded by a couple of men with rifles. Kyu had a very bad feeling about the whole setup and turned around before anyone at the *lodeu beullog* (roadblock) saw them. They walked back about a half a mile and then followed a small farmer's trail that took them through the next valley and past the roadblock without any NKPA observing them. Though it probably added a couple of hours to their travels, Kyu felt that it was the right decision. Only a few of the other refugees followed them. The rest continued blindly toward the roadblock.

South of Chonui, they did run into a bunch of soldiers that Kyu now recognized as Americans. Though they also had a *lodeu beullog* (roadblock), all that they did was briefly look through everyone's packs, pat them on the back, and let them continue on the road. Oh, there were a couple of young men that they pulled off to the side, but they appeared to be ROK deserters, and there were a couple of ROK soldiers there with them. When Kyu got to the roadblock, they asked him where he was from and where he was going. Kyu told them the truth—he was a simple *nongjangju* (farmer) from Taesŏng-tong and was headed south with his wife and daughter to get away from the North Koreans. The Americans liked Nabi and Sa-rang. They gave her something they called a chocolate bar. It had an interesting taste—very sweet but not very filling. Kyu would have rather gotten a rice ball or some kimchi. They did learn that the trains were still running in Choch'iwon and that many were able to climb aboard and ride further south. Maybe they could do that too. Nabi had an aunt who was at their wedding who lived in Taejon. Maybe they could stay there for a while until the North Koreans were stopped.

Once they passed one of the American vehicles that the others were calling a jeep. It was tipped on its side beside the road and was smoldering. When they walked by, Kyu could see four American bodies in the ditch beside it. They were blindfolded and had their hands tied behind their backs. Three also appeared to be bandaged and one had a red cross on his armband. There was a single bullet hole in the side of each of their heads. This was the first set of dead Americans that they had seen. Infiltrators or a North Korean patrol must have caught them by surprise and ambushed them somehow. By this time, the NKPA were dressing as refugees and holding their rifles under their clothing by their sides to infiltrate behind the lines. They were indistinguishable from normal refugees unless they were physically searched. Kyu thought he witnessed refugees that might have been soldiers from the North as they had very short hair. But to tie up the Americans that way and then kill them was not right.

They also saw planes flying up and down the highway. Behind them, they could see the planes diving from the sky at something on the ground. They were far enough away—the planes were north of Chonui—that they could not hear anything. They did see a lot of smoke come from that direction, so the planes must have bombed something.

They made it to Choch'iwon at about 1700 on 8 July after walking almost forty miles since the oxen and *Eomma* were killed outside of Suwon. It was a madhouse with refugees everywhere and soldiers from both the ROK and the Americans going here and there. They were able to get a small amount of diluted *baechu gook* (cabbage soup) outside a Christian church that refreshed them. They walked over to the rail yard and were surprised to find it guarded by American soldiers. It seemed that the trains coming north full of American soldiers were also full of mixed supplies for both the ROK and the Americans, and no one knew how to separate them, so they just took them off the trains and set them by the rail yard. Meanwhile, the Korean train conductors and engineers didn't want to stay this close to the NKPA. They wanted to get back south of Taejon where they felt safe. The Americans put armed guards in each of the locomotives to ensure that the engineers did not leave before the train was empty. Kyu and his wife climbed into a boxcar full of other refugees and hoped that the engineers would figure out a way to satisfy the Americans and start the train back south soon. But someone came by and said that the train would not leave until morning. So Kyu and his small family returned to the church where they received the diluted *baechu gook* (cabbage soup) to spend the night.

★ ★ ★

Meanwhile, the NKPA was marching steadily southward. At Chonui, the NKPA Third Division passed the NKPA Fourth Division after the battle. The Fourth Division then followed the westerly road behind the American Thirty-Fourth Regiment toward Kongju on the Kum River. The Third Division attacked the Americans south of Chonui. This was the first time that they battled American light tanks. They were no match for the larger T-34 tank, but they were effective against trucks and infantry. The NKPA destroyed two of the four American tanks, but the American Air Force caught part of the convoy out on the road and did heavy damage, including destroying several tanks.

Infiltrators and reconnaissance information provided the NKPA Third with detailed plans of the Twenty-First Infantry Third Battalion's defensive positions six miles north of Choch'iwon. In a surprise move at 0630 on 11 July, they launched a coordinated attack that started with an accurate mortar barrage that destroyed the command post, communications center, and most of the reserve ammunition. Approximately one thousand NKPA troops then performed their now-standard envelopment maneuver from both east and west while tanks and infantry attacked the middle. A number of roadblocks were then established behind the main attack that prevented evacuation of the wounded and resupplying. With those few coordinated maneuvers, they obliterated nearly 60 percent of the Third Battalion, and 90 percent of those who survived hobbled back to Choch'iwon without any weapons, ammunition, or canteens. A number returned shoeless and without helmets.

When General Dean learned what happened to the Twenty-First Regiment Third Battalion, he ordered the Third Engineer Combat Battalion to prepare every obstacle possible to defend Choch'iwon and to help cover the withdrawal of the remains of the Twenty-First Regiment. He also ordered the Nineteenth Infantry Regiment, Donnie's regiment, to Taejon from their positions in the south at Yonil.

After Task Force Smith and the battle at Osan, the Twenty-First Regiment First Battalion was reconstituted with untried replacements from other Third Army units from Japan. Colonel Smith rejoined it with his survivors from Osan. They built defensive positions about two miles north of Choch'iwon. At 0930 on 12 July, the NKPA executed a general envelopment movement against the First Battalion with two thousand soldiers. There were rumors that the NKPA used conscripted refugees, including women and children armed with pitchforks and shovels, to lead the attack. The Americans would not fire for fear of hitting the civilians until the regular NKPA were right on top of them. By then it was too late. They also started to perform an envelopment move, which was becoming their standard method of attack. At noon, Colonel Smith began disengaging from the NKPA by withdrawing company by company via truck. This retreat was orderly, and there was no pursuit. By 1600, the 325 soldiers remaining of the Twenty-First Regiment assumed positions on the south side of the Kum River across from Taep'yong-ni. Though it paid a very heavy price in men and materials, the Twenty-First Infantry Regiment had significantly delayed the two top NKPA divisions in a series of battles by three days.

Meanwhile, the Thirty-Fourth Regiment fought a number of delaying hit-and-run actions with the NKPA Fourth Division along the Kongju road to the west. Four light M24 Chaffee tanks joined the battalion, and a company from the Third Engineering Combat Battalion prepared bridge demolitions and mines along the route. Three of the four tanks were destroyed during the retreat. The Thirty-Fourth crossed the Kum and left a company on the north side of the river as a rear guard. General Dean was executing his last resort defensive positions to protect Taejon along the expansive shores of the Kum River.

6–12 JULY 1950,
YONIL, KOREA

When it rained in Missouri, it usually poured and then stopped. At Pusan during the monsoon, it seemed to rain steadily for hours on end. Donnie and the rest of Howe Company spent a day at the temporary Camp Hialeah in Pusan cleaning weapons, getting additional ammunition, and integrating the new soldiers into the company. The rumor mill was rampant. Everyone was still in good spirits and kept saying that the North Korean bandits would run at the sight of the mighty Chicks of the Nineteenth. The South Koreans all cheered and waved flags when they saw any of the troops, which also pumped them up. SFC Joseph Szito told them to ignore the cheering and get ready to pull out the next morning. They left Camp Hialeah and boarded a train at 1000 on 7 July for Taegu.

The Japanese built the main rail and highway in Korea, and it ran from Pusan through Taegu to Taejon and then on to Seoul. It was double-track most of the way but made of a narrow gauge. When loaded, the railcars tipped and swayed precariously, almost as bad as the LST crossing the Sea of Japan. Though the railcars were crowded, Donnie and the other troops could see out and were in good spirits. They passed a number of trains headed south toward Pusan. Each seemed to be loaded to capacity with ROK soldiers, civilians, and refugees. Donnie even saw goats and chickens on the laps of the southbound travelers. Many of the trains had refugees hanging outside onto the sides and roofs of the railcars. The main road where it followed the tracks was also jam-packed with refugees and army vehicles headed south. Everyone seemed to be headed south. What were they really getting into?

Howe Company traveled 104 miles by rail from Pusan to Taegu, arriving about 1900 on 7 July and bivouacked outside of the rail yard. There, eighteen additional soldiers were added from other Eighth Army units, taking their total on duty to 143. They also gained an assigned Deuce and a Half, a 2.5-ton truck, and driver to carry the heavy mortars and machine guns. While there, General Dean changed their orders. He directed them to proceed with haste toward Yongdok on the Korean east coast to provide defense for the Thirty-Fifth Fighter group stationed at Yonil six miles south of P'ohang-dong at the K-3 airport. The NKPA Fifth Division was heading south along the eastern coast and could take that strategic airport. Acquiring additional Korean drivers and vehicles, they drove one hundred miles east on the wet, slippery, unimproved road from Taegu to Yonil near the coast leaving early on 8 July. They were the only travelers on that east-west highway. They arrived at the Yonil airport early the next day, 9 July, at 0530, and immediately began creating defensive positions to protect it.

Korea at this time had very few improved highways. Most were unpaved old farm paths not wide enough for two cars to pass. The main north-south highway in the west paralleled the railway built by the Japanese. There were only a handful of airports in the entire country, and the North Koreans had already captured the major Kimpo and Suwon airports to the north. Yonil, though minor, could be improved and made into a base to provide the air force with a close-in airport for support. General Walker ordered General Dean to divert the Second Battalion of the Nineteenth Regiment to the east short-term until he could bring in more troops. Donnie's Howe Company was sent to Yonil to protect the airstrip there until additional troops could be sent to take over.

Donnie spent 9 and 10 July digging holes and filling sandbags with his squad to make defensible positions where their 81 mm mortar would have effective ranges of fire. They created three fixed locations ringed by sandbags and slit trenches facing toward the north and west at the edge of the runway. That way, they could move their mortar as needed and already knew the angle, range, and distances to marked targets from each location. It was hot, backbreaking work, and both days ended up dry and muggy. Though Donnie would never know it, the summer of 1950 turned out to be the hottest ever recorded in Korea. The only good thing was they got a hot meal each night instead of leftover World War II K rations. When they were not moving, they always got at least one hot meal.

They awoke the following day, 11 July, and went back to work digging and filling sandbags for the new defensive positions. Morale was still high, and Howe Company had yet to see an enemy, let alone fire a shot in anger. Donnie was quite proud of what they were able to build in two days. It should stop any band of North Korean bandits who might make it that far south. About noon, a number of one-and-a-half-ton trucks pulled into the airport. Parts of the First Cavalry and Twenty-Fifth Infantry Division arrived to relieve Howe Company at the airport and assume responsibility for defense of the east coast. Donnie looked for his friend from Seymour, Chuck Farr, who was assigned to the First Cavalry but didn't see him. Issuing Operations Instructions No. 1, General Dean had decided that he needed all three full regiments of the Twenty-Fourth Infantry Division to help defend Taejon and delay the NKPA advance. So they loaded Howe Company's equipment and truck onto a train with the rest of the battalion and left Yonil by 1530 on 11 July on their way back to Taegu.

They arrived in Taegu by train at approximately 0400 in the morning on 12 July. Taegu had changed in the few days they had been deployed in Yonil. General Walker transformed it into the command headquarters of the Eighth Army, and the town was now bustling with soldiers. Howe Company and the Nineteenth Infantry Second Battalion did not stay long. Instead, the railcars from Yonil were switched to another train and headed out that same morning toward Taejon. The weather was still hot and sticky, hitting almost 100°F. The inside of the train was almost unbearable. The GIs opened all the windows and leaned out as much as possible. That was when they first caught a glimpse of the impending onslaught. Passenger cars on the passing trains coming south from Taejon were full of wounded American soldiers. In many cases, they appeared to be seriously wounded. Other servicemen had joined the train in Taegu and told Donnie's company rumors of the battles fought by their sister regiments north of Taejon. Though they didn't have any real news, they told tales of major clashes and the many wounded and missing. That was the first inkling that Donnie and his company had that they might be entering into a real war and not just some puny police action. And they still had not fired live rounds through their mortar.

9–12 JULY 1950,
NEAR TAEJON, KOREA

About eighty refugees huddled in the boxcar from Choch'iwon with Kyu and his wife and daughter on the morning of 9 July. As the day was quite *deobgo deobda* (hot and muggy), they left the door open, providing some breeze as the train slowly chugged southward. Kyu felt lucky that they had a decent night's sleep at the little church and a simple breakfast. The pastor there spoke little Korean, but he described how best to get on the train and told them not to stop in Taejon but to continue all the way to Pusan if at all possible. He also gave them a small packed lunch and two canteens of water. He said that should provide them enough food for a day or so. That was the first time that Kyu had seen or used a *banhab* (canteen), but he thought it was much more practical than the wrapped clay jars that they had been using for water. Kyu offered the man some of his remaining ₩20,000 (won) in savings, but the man refused to take it. At that time, ₩20,000 was worth about $5. Kyu was just glad that they made it that far and were not still in Seoul.

Other refugees on board the train confirmed that the Reds were attempting to convert the citizens remaining in Seoul to communism. They said that 15,000 soldiers of the NKPA Eighteenth Division occupied Seoul. They were mixed Soviet, North Korean, and Chinese between eighteen and twenty years of age and were quite cruel. Remaining male and female residents between eighteen and thirty-six were forcibly conscripted into the NKPA with a goal of raising

450,000 additional soldiers. Everyone else was required to wear a communist badge on their left breast, and anyone caught without one was shot on sight. Water mains were shut off, and all rice purchases were controlled by the communists. By 8 July, the Reds had appointed a Supreme People's Committee to rule the surrounding area. The committee consisted of the mayor, police chief, chief prosecutor, chief judge, and other prominent-sounding officials. The communists filled all these positions with former ROK officials who defected. These included National Assembly members, director of internal affairs, minister of home affairs, members of opposition parties, and a former brigadier general. Soon, the communists sealed the city with no one allowed in or out, and deaths due to starvation increased dramatically.

Refugees swarm train

As they moved south, they passed another train heading north every hour or so. Most were mixed trains with passenger cars full of soldiers and then freight cars and flatbeds covered with all sorts of vehicles, many that Kyu couldn't recognize. Some, he now knew, were jeeps and large trucks. Other travelers told him that the other vehicles were light tanks and half-tracks. Kyu couldn't imagine what these vehicles could do, but surely, they must be able to stop the North Koreans. There appeared to be so many of them.

★ ★ ★

Though the troops of the Eighth Army in Japan were limited to World War II excess equipment at the beginning of the engagement, within a couple of weeks the magic of American logistics kicked in. The Pacific-Airlift that provided critical war equipment increased from 60 transport planes per day before the war to over 250 by 10 July. They were delivering all sorts of needed and unneeded equipment to the war fighters. Food for the war fighters was a problem with World War II K rations being the first, frontline food provided. But the miracle of logistics soon had nutritious C rations and five-in-one B rations in the hands of the front line, plus tons of frozen meat and vegetables for preparing hot food for delivery. World War II surplus ammunition was still normal during these early weeks with a large amount of it being defective. One mortar company reported that 40–50 percent of their illumination rounds did not work. All the ammunition created huge clouds of smoke when fired as these old munitions were not designed to be smokeless.

In contrast, the standard ROK ration at that time consisted of twenty-nine ounces of rice or barley, a half-pound of biscuit, and a half-pound of canned fish with spices. The rice was usually cooked and made into balls wrapped in cabbage leaves. They often soured before they made it to the frontline troops, if they made it there at all. Typically, the ROK commander this early in the war had to forage for food or purchase it locally for about ₩200 ($0.05) per soldier per day. So by this time, the ROK and GI food was mixed in the hot, stuffy boxcars headed toward the front. At Choch'iwon, it caused tremendous confusion as the GIs did not know what to do with the smelly and seemingly rotten cabbage and rice that was thrown in with their foodstuff. This was not ironed out until mid-September 1950 when standardized ROK rations were adopted, consisting of three meals of rice starch, biscuits, rice cake, peas, kelp, fish, and chewing gum packed into a waterproof bag weighing 2.3 pounds and providing 3,210 calories.

Other than the critical items flown in, the rest of the supplies needed by the army came in through the port of Pusan. By far, the best port on the Korean peninsula, it could handle at least twenty-four deepwater ships simultaneously, plus fourteen LSTs on its beaches. Thus, it could potentially handle forty-five thousand tons of freight daily; but shortages in labor, cranes, railcars, and trucks typically backlogged the flow of material out of Pusan and limited it to about fourteen thousand tons per day.

★ ★ ★

The railroad that Kyu and his family were riding on was the backbone of the distribution system within Korea. Built primarily by the Japanese during their occupation from 1910 through 1945, the main line was well ballasted and had at least two tracks from Pusan all the way to Seoul and beyond. Various spurs branched off this main line east and west, like the one that Donnie's Howe Company rode back from Yonil.

The twenty thousand miles of roadways in Korea on the other hand were a nightmare. Most were made of dirt with some crushed rocks and were less than eighteen feet in width. Numerous bottlenecks existed due to narrow bridges and bypasses where the width may drop to eleven to thirteen feet (twenty-two feet was the American standard for two-lane traffic). Sharp curves and grades up to 15 percent were common. Oxcarts, like Kyu's, were the predominant vehicles prior to the war and could traverse these roads with ease. American trucks and armor could not. Thus, at the onset, the railroad was the major way to move supplies, men, and equipment. And the North Koreans knew it.

Guerrillas attacked Kyu's train north of the Kum River. When they crossed over a small ravine, burp guns raked the cars from both sides of the railbed. Kyu and his family were away from the doors when the attack came. Many were not so lucky, and eighteen on the train were hit, seven of whom later died. Right after Kyu's car crossed the ravine, there were a couple of small explosions. The North Koreans threw hand grenades at the train causing confusion but little additional damage. The train engineer raced the train to get away. Kyu was glad that he did. They arrived in Taejon midafternoon on 12 July. That night, American demolitions blew up the rail bridges across the Kum River and the road bridges at Kongju and Taep'yong-ni the following morning. Kyu's train was one of the last to return south. Taejon was now isolated behind the moat of the Kum River.

13–15 JULY 1950, KUM RIVER, KOREA

Donnie s Howe Company and the rest of the Nineteenth Infantry Second Battalion arrived at Taejon in the late afternoon of 13 July. They unloaded their supplies and vehicles and drove fourteen miles northeast to Taep'yong-ni on the Kum River, arriving there about 0400 on 14 July. As the rest of the Nineteenth Regiment was already in defensive positions, Colonel Meloy held G Company and Donnie's H Company in reserve. Donnie and the rest of the mortars were located southwest of the regimental command post so that they could cover the curving shape of the river.

Taejon was considered a major crossroad and a rail center for South Korea. The Kum River protects it like a moat, winding around it in the shape of a big upside down letter *U*. About twelve miles to the northwest near the Yellow Sea, it is a mile or more wide. It then narrows into a river a few hundred yards across and loops northward. Kongju, where the Thirty-Fourth Regiment was located, was about twenty miles northwest of Taejon. Taep'yong-ni, where Donnie and the Nineteenth Regiment were at, was upstream about eight miles southeast. As the river had started its southerly course, Taep'yong-ni was only about fifteen air miles from Taejon, but the mountainous terrain made it closer to twenty road miles. The main rail bridge, now destroyed, crossed the Kum River east of Taep'yong-ni.

Based on Periodic Intelligence Report No. 2 and POW interrogations, General Dean knew that two crack NKPA divisions, the Third and the Fourth, were closing in on the Kum River from the north. Intelligence estimates put them at 60–80 percent full strength and accompanied by at least fifty tanks and forty to fifty artillery pieces. Scouting reports indicated that the NKPA were converging with many dressed in fatigues and helmets very similar in appearance to the Americans. In addition, the NKPA Second Division was currently moving south slightly to the east. It could join the attack on Taejon as well if they defeated the mixed ROK elements in front of them and made it through the rough mountains. Issuing Operations Instruction No. 3, General Dean positioned the Thirty-Fourth Regiment to the west along the Kum River guarding the Kongju approaches and replaced the Twenty-First with Donnie's Nineteenth Regiment to the east guarding the Taep'yong-ni and railroad bridges. He pulled the Twenty-First out to act as reserve and to be resupplied.

The Twenty-Fourth Division mobilized 11,440 men for the defense of the Kum River; 2,020 with the Thirty-Fourth to the west; 3,401 with the Nineteeth to the east; about 1,100 with the Twenty-First in reserve; and the remainder with the artillery, engineering, and support groups. General Dean ranked the Nineteenth Regiment at 96 percent combat efficiency, the Thirty-Fourth at 79 percent efficiency, and the Twenty-First at 40 percent as he prepared to defend the Kum River. In total, the Thirty-Fourth and Nineteenth Regiments guarded thirty-four miles of riverfront, which is a lot of ground to cover with two understrength regiments against two or possibly three crack enemy divisions.

The NKPA began their attack against the Thirty-Fourth to the west with their Fourth Division. Though expected to be at 60–80 percent full strength, they were actually at half their original strength. Less than six thousand men were active, supported by about twenty T-34 tanks and fifty pieces of artillery. Probes launched before midnight on 11 July located the UN force's dispositions and determined the width and depth of the Kum River. The air attacks at Chonui and P'yongt'aek had taught the NKPA not to mass in convoys during the day. So approaching the Kum River, the NKPA stayed camouflaged during the daylight and moved about at night. They also used more back roads and farm paths and stationed supplies in railroad tunnels and barns when possible. On 12 July, they positioned their units per the strategic plan developed from reconnaissance and spies.

The Third Battalion of the Thirty-Fourth Regiment arrayed four infantry companies with heavy mortars, approximately 140 men each, in defense of the Kum River at Kongju. The Sixty-Third Field Artillery Battalion supported it two to three miles to the south. The First Battalion of the Thirty-Fourth Regiment assembled in an area astride the road five miles south to act as reserve. Curriers provided the primary communications between the companies and battalions. By this time, the radio batteries were depleted with no replacements available, and there was little wire for telephones. The final company on the north side of the Kum River pulled back, and the road bridge across the Kum River at Kongju was blown by American engineers at 0400 on 13 July. By 0900, the NKPA established a machine gun and a tank on the northern end of the downed bridge. Only the seven hundred feet of the Kum River now separated the Thirty-Fourth from the NKPA. This so unnerved the composite K Company, which were made up of remnants from earlier battles, that the entire company retired to Taejon for medical evaluation. That left three companies to guard against the NKPA division to the north with no friendly units to the west and at least a two-mile gap between the Thirty-Fourth and the Nineteenth Infantry to the east.

The NKPA opened fire, probably with tanks, at the mortars behind the three remaining infantry companies guarding the river after daybreak on 14 July. Though the shells were airbursts, they did little damage. Lookouts reported that NKPA soldiers were crossing the Kum River in barges two miles to the west. Though informed of the landings, the artillery commander decided not to engage them to wait for bigger targets. He did request and received a Mosquito spotter plane to look for additional targets. About five hundred NKPA infantry crossed the Kum River before 0900 unopposed. The Mosquito spotter plane arrived and was driven away by a Yak fighter plane, but one artillery barrage was sent at the infantry crossing before it left. With the successful crossing, additional spotters became emplaced, allowing the enemy mortar and machine gun fire to become accurate on the westernmost company at Kongju. Its commander decided that their position was untenable with the NKPA infantry landings to the west. He pulled the entire company back all the way to the First Battalion and was subsequently relieved of command. Only two understrength infantry companies now guarded the Kum approaches at Kongju against a crack NKPA division.

Following standard NKPA tactics, the NKPA bombardment of these two infantry companies was a ruse to hold their attention. Simultaneously, the NKPA infantry that had crossed the river earlier attacked from the sides and rear. At 1430, wearing captured herringbone twill US fatigue uniforms, they first attacked the artillery position's outer perimeter machine gun nests two miles to the rear, capturing them intact and turning them against the artillery headquarters battery. Having precise intelligence, their first mortar round took out the artillery telephone switchboard. Additional shells hit the medical section, command post, radio truck, and an ammunition truck. Obviously, the NKPA mortar crews had fired live rounds previously. The NKPA Infantry then attacked the artillery's A Battery and B Battery in quick succession. Though everyone in the army is to be proficient with a rifle, only a few of the artillerymen grabbed theirs to fight back. The NKPA captured five 105 mm cannon intact with three thousand shells and destroyed five additional cannon and about eighty other vehicles. Over 135 GIs disappeared, listed as missing in action.

The Thirty-Fourth Regiment's reserve First Battalion was ordered to counterattack to recapture the guns and equipment. They started out after 1700 and marched in attack formation the two miles to the artillery site. They arrived at dusk and received sporadic machine gun fire. As it was getting dark, the commander ordered them back to their secure positions in the rear, blowing each bridge that they crossed in retreat. In what became a standard tactic for lost equipment, an air strike was called in to destroy the artillery site at dawn the next morning. Only three functional 105 mm cannon survived the NKPA attack. The two remaining Thirty-Fourth Regiment companies guarding the river sheepishly pulled back during the night, hiking over the mountains to rejoin the regiment.

The NKPA Fourth Division did not exploit their gains on 15 July. Though additional soldiers were ferried across the Kum River during the day, only two tanks made it across. The air force's strafing destroyed a number of boats but no tanks or artillery. The NKPA Fourth Division instead concentrated on consolidating and getting its equipment across the Kum before launching any further attacks. But the NKPA Third Division to the east had completed designing its strategy and was ready to attack. Donnie and the rest of Howe Company would soon find out what it was like to fire live ammunition.

12–15 JULY 1950,
TAEJON, KOREA

Ignoring the advice of the pastor at the church in Choch'iwon, Kyu and Nabi decided to get off the train in Taejon to find Nabi's aunt Sandara, whom Nabi thought was wise beyond belief. They knew that she owned a traditional *yagcho silang* (herbal market) specializing in red ginseng and other herbal medicines. She also was a *chimsula* (acupuncturist) and knew how to treat a body holistically. Though not really a doctor, she followed the teachings of Heo Jun and always tried to treat the cause of an illness and not just the symptoms. She also knew *tteum moxibustion* where a cone of burning *ssug* (mugwort) was held over a pressure point to stimulate and strengthen the blood. Nabi adored her, but Kyu had only met her at their wedding and then for only a short time. He was not sure what to think of her but knew that she was well-to-do.

★ ★ ★

Taejon on that twelfth of July was hot and muggy and seemed full of ROK and American soldiers and refugees from the fighting. The rail yard was much bigger than the one at Choch'iwon and many more workers were trying to sort out the freight on the trains. The sixth largest city in Korea, some 130,000 people called Taejon *jib* (home). It was a long and narrow city, straddling the north–south valley of the Taejon River at the western base of the Sobaek Mountains. *Non* (rice paddies) and farms lay to the north and west, and the extensive rail yard was located at its northeast corner. Besides the two tributaries of the Taejon River, the Yudung River flowed into the Taejon River two miles to the north of the city and then the Taejon River flowed into the Kap-ch'on River, which then joined the Kum River. In addition to the railroad, five main highways converged in Taejon. The airport was about three miles to the northwest across the Yudung River along the road to Kongju and along the route where the Thirty-Fourth Regiment deployed.

Nabi had never been to her aunt Sandara's and only knew that it was located in the good section of the city. When asked by Kyu, she wasn't even sure if it had a name or was just known as a *yagcho silang* (herbal market). So Kyu, Nabi, and the baby started walking in the same direction that most of the passengers were walking, which they hoped was toward the *sinae jungsim* (center of the city). After walking for about a half an hour, they finally came upon a *gyeong-gwan* (policeman). He said that there were three *yagcho silangs* in the city, but a woman fitting the description of Nabi's aunt Sandara ran the best one, and it was about four blocks west. Kyu almost had to hold Nabi back in her excitement to see if it indeed was the right place. When they got there, she burst into the store ahead of Kyu. When Kyu, who was carrying Sa-rang at the time, finally entered the store, he could see Nabi crying and hugging her aunt. She looked surprisingly like Nabi's mother now that she was in daily work clothing and not in wedding attire. Her aunt was glad but surprised to see them. She said that she had not heard from any of the family since the war began. She did not know anything about her sister, Nabi's mother, or her other family members.

Aunt Sandara lived above the store in an apartment that was quite opulent in Kyu's opinion. It had four main rooms, plus a bathroom with a real tub with running water. It also had electricity, but since the attack, that had become spotty. Her aunt was single but had a *namja hain* (manservant) who might also perform other duties. Aunt Sandara introduced him as Pak Him-chan. He looked about as strong as Kyu's oxen had been. Aunt Sandara politely asked Him-chan to go to the market area and get enough food supplies for travel for at least a week for four people. She then handed him a large sum of money.

While he was gone, Kyu had the luxury of taking a hot bath. Nabi and the baby, Sa-rang, took one after him. When they finished, they discovered that the manservant had returned with three large baskets of different types of food and some *maggeolli* (rice wine). They had a feast. It was the first cooked meal in three weeks that Kyu and Nabi had that was not eaten on the run. Nabi was just about asleep after consuming it. The baby was already sleeping. Sandara put them into a room she called the *gaegsil* (parlor) to rest. Even though he was dead tired, Kyu discovered that he did not need any red ginseng or *bosintang* (dog soup). It was the first time that he had been with Nabi since leaving Taesŏng-tong. They were both contented and slept well.

The next morning, 13 July, Aunt Sandara informed them that she had a *chim* (acupuncture) session this morning with the commander of the ROK First Division, Colonel Paik. He was in the city to discuss strategy with General Dean of the Americans. Remnants of the ROK Second Division, Capital Division, and First Infantry had combined and were deployed just north and east of Taejon and were battling it out with the NKPA Second Division. She handed Kyu ₩200,000 and told him to buy another set of clothing for both him and Nabi and to clean their current clothes while she met with the colonel and then come back in time for a late lunch. Kyu, Nabi, and Sa-rang did as she requested and returned around 1330 with new city garments instead of the farm clothes that they had been wearing. Kyu tried to return the extra ₩135,000 he didn't use buying clothes and doing laundry, but she told him to keep it. He did as he felt that they might need it later.

After lunch, Sandara filled them in on what the commander told her. He was quite glum. He felt that the Americans had great equipment, though nothing yet that could stop the NKPA tanks, but were not very brave. His First Division, on the other hand, was very brave but had little equipment and also had no way to stop the NKPA tanks. Confidentially, he felt that there was no way the ROK and Americans could stop the NKPA from taking Taejon maybe as early as 17 July. He recommended that they get out of Taejon as soon as possible. Having seen the brutality and commitment of the NKPA firsthand, Kyu agreed once he heard the colonel's opinion. Nabi just broke down and cried. Aunt Sandara declared that she would get them all tickets on a train to Pusan as soon as possible but doubted that any would be available today or tomorrow. She did not want to ride in a boxcar like Kyu and Nabi had getting to Taejon.

Nabi and the baby played in the apartment while Kyu and Aunt Sandara walked to the train station. As she suspected, all the reserved seats to Pusan were booked for both today and tomorrow. The earliest that they could get seats was on the 0900 train on 15 July. The *gichapyo* (train tickets) would only be valid for that train and the train company recommended that they be there at least two hours early to guarantee their seats. He also said that there was a very good chance that the train would be late. No refunds would be available if the train was canceled for any reason. Aunt Sandara bought the *gichapyo* (train tickets) with cash. As they were leaving, Kyu noticed a train that was unloading a large number of American soldiers and equipment. Though Taejon would forever be linked to them, this was the closest Woo Kyu-Chul would come to meeting Donald Eugene Matney as they both passed through the Taejon rail station at the same time on 13 July.

Kyu and Nabi went to bed early that evening and again enjoyed themselves. The next morning, 14 July, Kyu told Nabi to get the baby ready as he was taking them all on a gay tour of the city so that they could forget the war and just appreciate themselves. Aunt Sandara thought that was a splendid idea and had her manservant pack them a picnic lunch. They left the apartment and spent the day wandering around Taejon like tourists. Late in the afternoon before they got back to the apartment, they could see a large cloud of smoke to the north on the road to Kongju. With their interlude of peace complete, they returned to the apartment, somber in the realization that the war again was only a few miles north.

Kyu awoke at daybreak as normal on 15 July. He was surprised to find Him-chan, the *namja hain* (manservant), already up preparing a hearty breakfast. Him-chan suggested a large hot meal as another may not be available for quite some time. Kyu went in to wake Nabi, but she was already feeding Sa-rang. How he loved the sight of his wife breastfeeding their daughter! Nabi had their packs ready. Aunt Sandara called from the kitchen and gave Kyu ₩700,000 and a couple of bags of food and snacks. She said to be sure to spread the money and food between each of their packs and maybe hide some on Sa-rang since one could never tell what would happen during a journey in wartime. When they went downstairs to the store, Kyu was surprised to see the shelves empty. Aunt Sandara hid anything of value that she did not pack. She put a Closed sign on the window and double-locked the door. She was sad and concerned that she would never see her shop again.

Him-chan, the *namja hain* (manservant), had arranged for a *mal-i kkeuneun macha* (horse-drawn carriage) to take them and their baggage to the train station. They made it there by 0705. When they got there, it was a madhouse. The train status board listed all the northbound departure trains as Canceled and the southbound trains as Delayed. When asked, one harried *jihwija* (conductor) replied that North Korean airplanes had attacked the trains to the south, the Americans blew up the bridges to the north, and he didn't know how long it would be until anything would be fixed so that trains could arrive. They waited in the chaos of the train station until after 1400 when a train finally chugged into the station from the south. The stationmaster walked over to the status board and quickly changed the status for the 1220 train to Boarding and the 0900 to Canceled. Kyu thought that Aunt Sandara would have a heart attack. Him-chan, however, immediately went over to the ticket window and shook the ticket vendor's hand. The latter looked at it and then slowly nodded and exchanged their tickets from the 0900 train to the 1220 train. Kyu, Nabi, the baby, Aunt Sandara, and Him-chan all climbed aboard a general passenger car with their luggage in tow at 1538. It looked like they would be leaving Taejon soon.

14–16 JULY 1950,
NEAR TAEP'YONG-NI,
KOREA, ON THE KUM RIVER

Due to the Kum River meanderings, the Nineteenth Infantry defended fifteen air miles of front line covering over thirty miles of riverbank. That was a lot of territory to defend with a two-battalion regiment. Luckily, the Kum River this 14 July ran six to fifteen feet deep and two to three hundred yards wide with a strong current from the monsoonal rains. The NKPA could not wade it or take tanks across without help. The steep riverbanks also ranged from four to eight feet high. To cross heavy equipment, the NKPA would require boats or barges or a reconstructed bridge. Colonel Meloy deployed his troops the best that he could, subject to the terrain and limited availability. He placed E Company to the far right (east) between the destroyed rail bridge and another tributary emptying into the Kum from the north. He placed C Company and A Company two miles from E Company astride the main road through Taep'yong-ni with a thousand-yard gap between them. B Company was located adjacent to the west of A Company. A five-mile gap to the west before the boundary with the Thirty-Fourth Infantry was guarded by a single platoon from G Company. He located the command and artillery regiments in the center about a mile or so south of the river. The Second Battalion—composed of F, G, and Donnie's H Company—was held in reserve behind the command post. Three batteries of artillery were also deployed to support the Nineteenth, and Chaffee light tanks were expected to arrive later that day. As the day was clear and visibility good, Colonel Meloy directed air strikes against eleven enemy tanks on the north shore that were spotted, but they were dug in well enough that only one appeared to be damaged. The NKPA soldiers and tanks respected the power of the air force.

As air spotters and shared radio frequencies were not yet prevalent, friendly fire accidents did happen between ground and air forces. About 1330, three P-51 fighter planes with South Korean markings came out of the sun and strafed the artillery C battery. They also dropped three bombs; two of which did not explode. Luckily there were no injuries. The bomb disposal squad disarmed the two duds. After this incident, violet and other colored panels were placed on all vehicles to help friendly planes identify them from the air.

Colonel Meloy learned of the collapse of the Thirty-Fourth Regiment late that afternoon. This meant that his entire left flank was now exposed. The G Company guard platoon reported apparent NKPA crossings to their west; they engaged with mortars and machine guns, and the enemy returned to the north shore. Colonel Meloy ordered Lieutenant Colonel Thomas McGrail to form a task force to guard this exposed northwest flank. Colonel McGrail pulled in the remainder of G Company and most of Howe Company, two Chaffee light tanks, and two quad-50 Meat Choppers (M16A1), which are self-propelled antiaircraft vehicles, that had just arrived. As part of the assigned Howe Company mortar crews, Donnie Matney would first taste combat as part of Task Force McGrail.

First thing on the morning of 15 July, SFC Joseph Szito yelled to the machine gun and mortar crews to load the Deuce and a Half trucks allocated to them. They quickly gathered their packs, equipment, rifles, and ammunition and got on board. Driving in a small convoy, they set out southwest from the command post and joined with G Company and a couple of tanks and quad-50s. They bounced and rolled across the hilly terrain for about two miles, then turned north and set up defensive positions along the banks of the Kum River, just past a large river bend near a hamlet known as Sangwang-ni. G Company deployed to the east at the river bend, and H Company spread out along the river. Donnie and the other mortar crews set up defensive positions behind a small hill that gave them some protection from counterfire spotters. The position provided a good range of fire of the entire river covering both companies. Their spotter stayed on top of the hill and could see quite a distance all along the river. Colonel McGrail placed one of the Chaffee tanks and a quad-50 on each side of the small task force. Once in position, he had the tanks and the mortars open fire on the small village and hovels on the north side of the river.

Donnie and his mortar crew fired their first live rounds that afternoon. It took them a number of rounds to walk the fire onto the location desired by their spotter, but pretty soon, they got the hang of it and were firing two to three shots per minute with few requested corrections. *Thump, boom. Thump, boom. Thump, boom.* The NKPA just hunkered down as the air force was also bombing and strafing any position where they saw movement. During this initial engagement, PFC Lorenzo Alarcon was accidentally wounded by friendly fire while setting up a defensive machine gun nest. He was evacuated by jeep to the field hospital in Taejon. Other than that, Donnie and the rest of Howe Company received little return fire, and there were no other incidents during those first few hours of battle.

81mm Mortar and Crew

Sporadic firing by Donnie and the mortars and the machine guns continued until early evening. Occasionally, the NKPA would fire back, but the mortar crew and machine guns would quickly silence them. Word came down from Colonel Meloy to expect a major enemy attack during the night. SFC Joseph Szito issued the mortar crews illumination rounds and said to randomly fire them from the different mortars throughout the night so that the infantry could watch for enemy boats.

The NKPA started their attempt to cross the Kum River after dark. Machine gun and recoilless rifle fire repelled three tries to cross the river in front of C Company. Donnie and the other 81 mm mortars also fired and helped repel them to the west. A few of the 81 mm mortar rounds misfired, fell short, and knocked out two of C Company's close support 60 mm mortars. Luckily, no one was hurt. No NKPA made it across the Kum River during the early evening hours. But it was a dark, moonless night, and the NKPA still had plenty of time to attack.

Suddenly at 0300 on Sunday, 16 July, an enemy plane flew over the Kum and dropped a bright flare. With that signal, the entire NKPA Third Division opened fire on the Nineteenth Regiment. Colonel Meloy commented that the intensity of fire was greater than any he ever experienced from the Japanese during World War II. Under cover of this intense barrage, the NKPA used boats and rafts and started swimming across all along the banks of the Kum. The 155 mm howitzers behind the command post fired the flares for the eastern flank. At this critical junction, they were delayed. The NKPA exploited this darkness and landed a large number of troops in the eastern gap between C and E Companies. In their standard maneuver, they overran one platoon of C Company, then used that gap to bring in larger concentrations of infantry and performed an envelopment maneuver to attack the command post and heavy mortar platoons in the rear. They also sent a large contingent to establish a roadblock in the rear to stymie reinforcement and retreat. Simultaneously, thirty to forty infantrymen at a time swam across the Kum west of B Company, and by 0700, an estimated five hundred NKPA soldiers managed to cross the river. They continued south and seized the high country above the command post. Colonel Meloy rallied cooks, mechanics, clerks, a Chaffee tank, and an M16A1 quad-50 and led a counterattack at 0900 that successfully drove off the enemy. They didn't realize that most of these NKPA didn't retreat but instead moved to the roadblock in their rear.

During the night, Donnie and Task Force McGrail also fired at numerous enemy crossing attempts and successfully stopped all of them in their sector. Donnie's crew must have fired at least two hundred live mortar rounds during the night. "I'd never experienced combat. The unknown, the uncertainty, every whisper, every crack of a leaf… It's just startling, you don't know what to expect."[15] Three buddies in a machine gun nest were wounded by the enemy. But the main enemy force had already infiltrated east of them, and like with the

---

15   Ent, *Fighting on the Brink: Defense of the Pusan Perimeter*

Thirty-Fourth a day before, they were attacking the rear artillery positions.

The NKPA roadblock in the rear of the command post blocked the only road to Taejon from Meloy's command post, and American resupply vehicles and ambulances piled up on each side of it. The NKPA chose a perfect location for the roadblock where the road wound through a valley between two hills that effectively obstructed the view through it. They set up at least six machine gun nests on the hills above the road, adding additional troops to guard its flanks as the day went on. The Americans thought at the time that they had at least six tanks embedded in the roadblock, but that was not true. Colonel Meloy drove over to observe it about noon. When he tried to rally troops to counterattack, he was wounded in the calf of a leg. Lieutenant colonel Otho T. Winstead assumed command and contacted General Dean, requesting help from Taejon to break the roadblock from the south. General Dean replied that it would be at 1530 before help could arrive. Colonel Winstead then ordered the regiment to begin withdrawing.

Troops began to withdraw in organized fashion company by company. That day was particularly hot and sticky—passing 100°F and close to that in humidity. It was hard for the tired and out of shape infantrymen to stay sharp during the withdrawal. And the roadblock was still a major problem. As elements of the First Battalion reached it, they fired from higher ground to the west but could not locate the enemy machine gun nests. The NKPA used smokeless gunpowder and were well camouflaged, so the GIs could not see them. The Americans used gunpowder that smoked, so the enemy could easily identify where a shot originated and effectively return fire. The GIs mounted another counterattack, but a flight of P-51 Mustangs fired on them by mistake, and the counterattack fell apart. F Company in reserve was supposed to help in these situations, but it was cut off and surrounded by the enemy and unable to help break the roadblock.

Finally, a runner made it to Task Force McGrail. Colonel McGrail took the two tanks and quad-50s and started toward the roadblock from the far side at about 1530. He met up with General Dean and his small relief force, including two additional quad-50s south of the roadblock. Colonel McGrail then drove toward the roadblock with a tank in front, the four quad-50s loaded with infantry, and a tank in the rear. When they came into a straight part of the road, the

NKPA attacked. Since they could not locate the smokeless NKPA machine gun nests, the tanks returned fire with little effect. The NKPA machine guns destroyed the four quad-50s, and 90 pecent of the accompanying infantrymen were wounded. When they ran out of ammunition, the tanks withdrew without attempting to clear the roadblock from the south side. Removing the roadblock from the south did not work.

At 1600, the wounded Colonel Meloy loaded into the last tank on the north side of the roadblock. After four attempts, the tank successfully pushed the vehicles blocking the road out of the way and rumbled southward. About twenty vehicles followed it, taking continuous enemy fire and wounding additional during the drive through the mile-length melee of the roadblock. Seeing what happened to the previous vehicles, the remaining one hundred vehicles and five hundred men still trapped on the north side did not brave this shooting gallery. At about 1700, the major now in charge after Colonel Winstead was killed ordered all the vehicles destroyed and the men to hike over the mountains to Taejon.

To say the hike out from behind the roadblock was torturous would be an understatement. But the last of the five hundred men headed into the mountains by 2100, and the remaining vehicles were set on fire or otherwise destroyed. A group of about thirty wounded had to be hand-carried on litters. Litter bearers in that heat climbing into the hills kept dropping out. Finally, at the top, no one could carry the wounded any farther. A corpsman and a clergyman volunteered to stay with them until help could come back. Guerrillas from the NKPA found them first. The clergyman tried to protect them. They shot and killed them all, except the corpsman who hid and escaped on foot to report the atrocity.

Meanwhile to the west, Howe Company and the rest of the remaining infantry in Task Force McGrail waited for trucks to arrive from the airport. While they waited, SFC Joseph Szito had Donnie and the squad load the mortars and heavy machine guns onto the assigned Deuce and a Half company truck. When the trucks from the airport finally arrived, Howe and Golf Companies departed farther west approximately seven miles where they ran into additional NKPA. They dismounted and a short intense battle ensued. They were successful in stopping the enemy's flanking movement. While there, they rescued members from the routed Thirty-Fourth Regiment's artillery, including James W. Bolt[16]. When they approached the Kongju-Taejon road north of the airport, they encountered a jeep with the hood up on the far side of a bridge across a small stream. The lead jeep of the small convoy waved as they drove up, thinking that the jeep guarding the bridge was part of the Thirty-Fourth Infantry protecting the approaches to Taejon. The driver of the jeep called out in perfect English that it was safe to cross the bridge. Suddenly the jeep opened fire using a mounted .50-caliber machine gun hidden behind the raised hood. The convoy screeched to a stop, and the infantry troops leaped into battle. They quickly dispatched the enemy troops on the jeep and in the surrounding brush at the roadblock. Donnie and the mortar crew dismounted but did not participate in the short, intense battle. They remounted and headed toward Taejon. When they drove past the dead NKPA troops manning the jeep, Donnie noticed that they were all dressed in captured American uniforms. These villains did not believe in the Geneva Convention and the rules of war!

Three additional machine gunners from Howe Company were wounded during the day's battles. All the buck privates in the entire Nineteenth Regiment were promoted to private first class,[17] including Donnie. The Nineteenth Regiment awarded over eighty medals for valor, including sixteen Distinguished Service Crosses, for heroic actions during the battle of the Kum River, more than in any other battle. Donnie fired his first live rounds, and some of his friends were wounded. The company morning reports stated this about the day's activities: "Moved 7 miles South fr Kum River to stop enemy flank attack; destroyed 1 roadblock & successfully fought off flank attack."[18] In perspective, the sister Heavy Mortar Company fired 1,588 rounds during that twelve-hour period. What a way to start a police action. They retreated thirty miles in their small convoy that day through Taejon and Okch'on, then south to Yongdong to reorganize and rearm. General Dean planned to use Yongdong as the next location for a delaying battle.

---

16 We received an e-mail from Mr. Bolt telling us about his rescue.

17 Per order dated 9 July from the adjutant general, promotions were limited due to army budget constraints.

18 H Company Nineteenth Infantry morning report dated 16 July 1950.

The date 16 July was a black day for the Nineteenth Regiment. Of the 3,401 deployed to fight at the Kum River, 650 (19%) were casualties. Almost all its artillery and heavy equipment was lost, destroyed at the roadblock between the hills. Only two rifle companies (E and G) escaped unscathed. Donnie's Howe Company had seen action and successfully engaged the enemy, but seven were wounded. The Nineteenth needed Yongdong to regroup.

15–17 JULY 1950,
TAEJON, KOREA

Kyu and his family sat on the train from 1538 until almost 2200 on 15 July. They ate from their meager store of food and used the facilities on the train even though they just dropped onto the tracks below. Then suddenly a group of American and ROK soldiers came on board and ordered everyone off. This train was needed to transport wounded soldiers back to Pusan. At that time, the worst wounded cases were flown by air when possible to Japan for treatment. The more ambulatory ones, once stable, traveled by truck or train to hospitals behind the lines. Flying wounded in helicopters and close to the action mobile army surgical hospitals (MASH) would not be implemented for several more months.[19] Kyu noticed casualties from both the Twenty-Fourth Infantry and the ROK combined forces lined up outside of the train car. Most wore bandages, and many were held by friends. A few were on litters or portable beds with medics in attendance. But there were also quite a few Americans who appeared to have no obvious injuries. Kyu and his small band of weary travelers grabbed their luggage and reluctantly got off the train. Once everyone was off, it was sad to see how many of the soldiers with no apparent injuries rushed onto the train to grab seats. None seemed interested in helping the walking wounded or others who needed help. *"Geobjaeng-i,"* (Cowards) said Him-chan. Sandara politely

---

19   The 8055 MASH unit did offer General Dean their services in a memorandum dated 11 July 1950.

corrected him and said that they all appeared to be shell-shocked[20]. "Same thing," said Him-chan.

As it was already late and the train ticket window was closed, Kyu suggested that they just sleep on the floor of the station. That way, they would hear if any other trains came into the station late and may be able to get on it. Aunt Sandara would have none of it. She wanted to go home to the store and her apartment. That late and with the war on, there were no taxis or porters or any sort of for-hire transportation at the station. A walk all the way to Sandara's store and apartment would be difficult with the luggage during the day, let alone at night. Him-chan thought that they would be perfect targets for *dodug* (thieves) if they tried to walk. Sandara remembered a boarding house nearby. The owners were customers of hers. They wearily trudged over to it with their luggage. Luckily, there was one room left with two beds in it. Kyu and Nabi took one with little Sa-rang at Nabi's feet. Him-chan and Sandara took the other even though they were not married. Kyu thought he heard a lot of rustling coming from them after they went to bed. He was too tired, and Nabi was already asleep to try any rustling of their own.

At 0700 on Sunday, 16 July, Sandara gave Him-chan money and politely asked him to look for food for both today and for travel. She said that they would wait at the boarding house until he returned no matter what. While Him-chan was away, Kyu walked the short distance to the railroad station. It was still packed with people hoping to get onto a train. There weren't any trains in the rail yard at that time. Even though it was after 0800, the status board listed all the departure trains northbound as Canceled and all the southbound trains as Delayed. More ominous, the ticket window was closed. Kyu glumly walked back to the boarding house.

Him-chan returned from his shopping at about 1045. He had only one small bundle and not much money left. He reported most of the markets were closed. The few that were opened had heard that at least one of the American brigades had been destroyed, and there wasn't anyone left to stop the NKPA from taking all Taejon. Though not entirely true, the few shopkeepers who opened quadrupled their prices for their wares. Him-chan had bought only what he thought was needed to replace what they already had eaten and then some other

---

20 *Shell-shocked* was the term used then for post-traumatic stress disorder.

small food items that would keep and were easy to carry. He also said that the streets were crowded with refugees starting to head south on foot. Kyu told him about the ticket office being closed. Him-chan said that possibly the ticket window salesman hadn't shown up for work, but he doubted that they could get reserved seats on any train that did make it in without the army taking them away. Their options were limited. Though Sandara had money, the probability of getting valid train tickets were now slim. They could crowd into a boxcar and hope for the best, but Kyu reminded them of the attack when they arrived. There were few automobiles or trucks running that the army hadn't already preempted and no gasoline available if there were. They might be able to hire or buy a horse or oxcart. They could start walking, or they could hunker down in Sandara's apartment and hope for the best. After discussing it and eating a small meal from their meager supplies, they decided to stay at the boarding house one more night. Kyu would go to the train station and hurry back to get them if a train arrived or the ticket office reopened while Him-chan would see if he could hire or purchase a horse or oxen wagon. Sandara went to her customer, the boarding house owner, to see if they could stay another night. She said yes for triple the previous night's rate.

Kyu went to the train station to check if any trains came in that they could possibly board. When he got there, he wasn't surprised to discover that the ticket office was still closed and the train status board unchanged. The number of people waiting for a train had grown. A train did finally arrive in the early evening of 16 July. Hundreds of refugees crowded around it, clamoring to get on board. However, a mixture of ROK and American soldiers held them back. Kyu was surprised to see a number of well-dressed Americans soldiers coming to board the train. The other soldiers all stood straight and saluted them as they went past. Except for about four staff officers, General Dean ordered the evacuation of the headquarters command of the Twenty-Fourth Division by train that night to travel to Yongdong, eighteen miles to the south, to make preparations for the next delaying-action battle. No refugees were allowed on the train. Kyu returned to the boarding house dejected. Him-chan was there without a wagon or any form of transportation.

They spent the night in the boarding house without incident and got up the next day, Monday, 17 July. Him-chan again went out in search of transportation and additional foodstuff that they could take on their journey south. Kyu went back to the train station. The girls stayed at the boarding house. They all said that they would meet back there by 1300. Kyu hoped that Him-chan would be successful as he had few expectations of getting a reserved seat on a train.

The train station looked exactly like it had when he had left it the previous evening. The status board still showed all northbound trains as Canceled and southbound trains as Delayed. The ticket office was closed. Hundreds of refugees milled about. However, there was a train pulled in the yard with soldiers guarding it. An official-looking Korean was also standing out by the train with a cigar in his mouth and a watch in his hand. Kyu thought it wouldn't hurt to ask him if he knew anything. So he walked to him in his new city clothes and asked if he knew whether or not the train would be taking on any passengers. He just laughed and said that this was war and the soldiers now controlled all the trains. This one would be full of more wounded headed back to Pusan and would be pulling out in half an hour or so. They might be able to scramble into a boxcar once they were unloaded if the army would let them, but they would have to be ready to go soon. He also said that he had heard that this will be the last train coming as all the others were now stopping in Yongdong since the commanding officers had moved there. He also did not think that Taejon would be in friendly hands much longer.

Kyu rushed back to the boarding house. It was about 1230 on 17 July, and Him-chan was already back empty-handed. He said what cost four times as much yesterday was now ten times as much and only five markets were open. No one had any horses or oxen available. He did purchase a *sonsule* (handcart). They hurriedly loaded their luggage into the *sonsule* (handcart) and rushed off to the rail station. When they got there a little before 1300, they were relieved to see that the soldiers were still unloading the boxcars. The passenger cars were already full of wounded, some again not looking very hurt. The group of five joined the crowd of refugees waiting to see if they could climb aboard the boxcars.

17–18 JULY 1950,
YONGDONG, KOREA

Lieutenant Reagan flipped out after the Kum River. There was no other easy way to describe it—not that anyone could blame him. Here they came from peaceful Japan for a police action all cocky and sure that the North Koreans would flee at the sight of the mighty Chicks, and instead, they were nursing their seven wounded twenty miles away from an enemy who appeared to be stronger and better prepared. It was enough to drive any sane commander crazy. He was only a lowly first lieutenant and not even a captain, and they expected him to lead over 130 men into combat. He just kept asking himself what they could have done better.

They may be in a war and not a police action, but by God, their paperwork had to be completed. Luckily, Warrant Officer Herbert Worzel[21] covered for Lieutenant Reagan by taking over the administrative duties for the company, including writing and signing daily reports. SFC Joseph Szito just ignored Lieutenant Reagan like normal and tried to keep Donnie and the troops active by teaching them better ways to survive combat. They cleaned their rifles, and this time, everyone did it and made darn sure that the sergeant approved the results. They also received additional ammunition, including new rounds for the mortar. SFC Joseph Szito also picked up a M1911A1 .45-caliber pistol and web belt, which usually only officers

---

21   WO Herbert Worzel died on 20 September 1950 in Tokyo General Hospital of wounds unrelated to battle. He is not listed as a Korean War casualty.

wore. He gave it to Donnie as he heard that the NKPA liked to attack the mortar crews. The sergeant thought someone on the mortar crew should have one just in case.

Yongdong was on the main railroad line, so trains and supplies came regularly. Not many trains went farther north toward Taejon as the Twenty-Fourth divisional headquarters had been moved there. General Dean planned to withdraw the remaining troops from Taejon to Yongdong on 19 July. SFC Joseph Szito ordered troops to dig slit trenches and sandbag positions for the mortars and machine guns with crossing fields of fire. These preparations would make Yongdong defensible for the next delaying action. And unlike when they were in Japan, they actually

H Company morning report on 15 July 1950

had to stand on guard duty for real. They did receive hot meals on 18 July for the first time since Yonil.

Rumors in the trenches were rampant. Supposedly, General Walker and the rest of the Eighth Army were deploying in Pusan to the south. The First Cavalry was coming to relieve the battered Twenty-Fourth Division. The Thirty-Fourth Regiment was being disbanded due to its poor performance. The North Koreans would be attacking here tomorrow. No one knew what to believe. SFC Joseph Szito just worked Donnie and the squads harder on that Tuesday, trying to get them to think like soldiers and make defensive preparations for anything that might happen.

New replacements[22] did arrive for the companies of the Nineteenth. Though these tenderfoots wouldn't know the history of the regiment or have any real friends, everyone was glad to have additional help building defenses. They were added piecemeal to each company within the regiment instead of creating a new third battalion. Most were treated as pariahs as the existing soldiers did not want to get close to someone inexperienced who might not last long once the fighting restarted. The new personnel also meant General Dean hadn't given up on them yet. But it also meant that they would be back in battle soon.

Donnie wasn't sure whether to like or dislike one squad of soldiers that came through Yongdong. They were gravediggers and mostly Negro soldiers. Howe Company had been told that Korea would be the first war where if you died, you would automatically be returned home to America for burial instead of being interred in an anonymous graveyard in Korea. In every other war, the dead were buried close to the battlefield and returned home after the war only if relatives insisted. But President Truman decided that it would be better to bring home the dead for proper burial and for closure for the families since Korea was a police action and not declared a war. Donnie cynically supposed that Truman really thought that returning the dead home would help him gain more votes. He was not sure if Truman thought that the votes would come from the grateful families or from the dead. Taejon had a temporary GI cemetery already, but supposedly these troops were going to dig them up and take the bodies back to America. Donnie wasn't sure if that was a good thought or a bad one. He knew his mother, Willa, would like it better if he was buried in Seymour, Missouri, instead of some place in Korea if he happened to die. But he would be dead and probably wouldn't know the difference.

Meanwhile, the Twenty-Fourth Infantry Division command evaluated the situation after the Kum River battle. The 17 July Periodic Intelligence Report summarized the NKPA tactics seen at the Kum River as follows:

It is definitely established that the enemy, before executing a frontal attack, will generally infiltrate

---

22 General Dean requested sixty-three officers, fourteen warrant officers, and six hundred ten enlisted in a replacement requisition dated 10 July prior to the Kum River battle.

the rear areas, establish roadblocks, and attempt to destroy our artillery in a great many cases ignoring the infantry until this has been accomplished.[23]

It concluded that "it is likely that the enemy has succeeded in moving sufficient strength in infantry, artillery and armor across the Kum River to attack with vastly superior strength at points of his own choosing."[24] Based on this assessment, General Dean issued Operations Instruction No. 7 to withdraw from Taejon and regroup at Yongdong for the next delaying battle.

General Walker, head of the Eighth Army, flew to Taejon before noon on 18 July to meet with General Dean. They met at the airport northwest of town. General Dean had consolidated the artillery at the airport and some elements of the Thirty-Fourth Infantry were on the road from Konju nearby. General Walker explained that he needed the Twenty-Fourth Division to hold Taejon for at least two more days. General Dean's prior plans to evacuate the remaining Thirty-Fourth Infantry troops from the south of Taejon to Yongdong to make another defensive stand there instead of at Taejon would have to be countermanded. General Walker wanted the Twenty-Fourth Division to hold on to Taejon longer to provide the First Cavalry time to move up to the front and allow him more time to create a defensible position that would become known as the Pusan Perimeter. General Dean rescinded Operations Instruction No. 7. He ordered the recall of the Nineteenth from Yongdong that afternoon and deployed the remains of the Twenty-First Regiment as his reserve force to the railroad tunnels south of Taejon at Okch'on. The plan sounded surprisingly like what happened to the Nineteenth Regiment way back in the Civil War at the Chickamauga River—they were being tasked to take a stand so that the rest of the army could dig in better defensive positions farther away.

---

23 Nineteenth Infantry Journal "Periodic Intelligence Report No. 6" dated 17–1800 July 1950 declassified 8 December 2009.

24 Nineteenth Infantry Journal "Periodic Intelligence Report No. 6" dated 17–1800 July 1950 declassified 8 December 2009.

General Walker and General Dean at Taejon airport

While the two generals were meeting at the airport, the NKPA fired shells at the artillery on the field and pockmarked the runway. A transport plane carrying critical supplies noticed the scarred runway and announced it was returning to Pusan. The story goes that General Dean himself got on the radio and told the pilot that if he did not land, he would shoot the plane down himself. The plane landed and off-loaded quickly and then took off again for the safety of Japan. Among its critical supplies were the first twelve 3.5-inch bazookas capable of stopping a T-34 tank.

Late in the afternoon of 18 July back in Yongdong, Donnie heard explosions and random rifle fires. Donnie and the squad jumped into the trenches. An NKPA scouting patrol launched a couple of mortar rounds into camp just to remind the Americans that they were not welcome. Unluckily, PFC Alberto Scheiler was wounded and had to be evacuated by train to Pusan. A squad went after them, but the NKPA melted into the background of refugees on the main road from Taejon. That meant that there were now eight wounded from Howe Company. Only 135 remained fit for combat out of 145 assigned to the company. They received word that evening that they would be returning to Taejon early the next morning. They did get another hot meal that evening. Sergeant Szito ordered them to have everything packed ready to depart by daybreak. They had received two nights of rest and respite while building future defensive positions and were heading right back into battle where the fortifications would be limited. Maybe someone else would appreciate their efforts and use those positions against the NKPA later.

17–18 JULY 1950, TAEJON, KOREA

Kyu and his weary band of refugees waited and waited to board the train that Monday afternoon on 17 July. The soldiers directed about eighty refugees to climb aboard each of the empty boxcars, taking time to search each refugee. They made sure that each group had water and at least a little bit of food before letting them aboard. Most did, but some were turned away. Kyu did some rough counting and it became clear to him that they would not make it onto this train unless most of the refugees in front of them were unprepared. Some of those who were turned away went over to the other side of the tracks and climbed on the top of the boxcars to ride outside. Kyu knew that Nabi's aunt Sandara would never agree to that. Finally, the soldiers said that the train was full and started directing the remaining refugees back into the station. Nabi started to cry, but Sandara just said not to worry, there would be another train. They went back into the station to wait.

Just then, Kyu noticed a poorly dressed *nongbu* (peasant) off to the side with a *baenang* (backpack) who looked just like his older cousin on *Eomma's* side of the family from Wonsan in North Korea. Kyu hadn't seen him since the wedding. Why would he be here? Kyu got up without telling any of the others what he was doing and started walking toward him. As he got closer, he was more convinced that it really was his cousin. When he was about ten feet from him, Kyu called out his name. His cousin looked wide-eyed and suddenly lowered his head and started walking rapidly away. Kyu wondered why he did not want to greet him. He started after him but lost him in the crowd. Kyu returned back to his family and told them what had happened. Him-chan said it was most likely that his cousin was now a spy for the North Koreans, scouting out the defenses of Taejon and trying to determine what military was coming and going on the trains.

The North Koreans had thousands of guerrillas and spies infiltrated into South Korea before the war. Many were from the North, but quite a few were South Koreans sympathetic to the idea of communism. They had a sophisticated network to get information back to North Korea and the army. At this stage of the invasion, North Korea knew more about the American troop disposition and strength than General Dean.

Aunt Sandara agreed that they should stay at the rail station that night so as not to lose their place in the refugee queue waiting to board a train. Him-chan and Kyu refilled their water containers and looked for additional food but didn't find any. There were no additional food vendors around the train station. All of them had closed and left, so they dipped further into their meager supplies. That night, they all slept restlessly on the floor of the train station. One small train did arrive, but it was full of war materials and was quickly dispatched by the soldiers. No refugees were allowed on it for the return trip southbound.

Tuesday, 18 July, was just like the day before at the rail station—more refugees, no food, and only two trains that didn't take any refugees south. Rumors were rampant—that the North Koreans would be there that evening was one of them, another one was that the airport had been shelled, and the third had the Americans pulling out of Taejon that evening.

★ ★ ★

After his meeting with General Walker, General Dean updated his plans to delay the NKPA by staying in Taejon another day and blocking the five main roads. The Thirty-Fourth Regiment would be the primary defense along the two northern routes. The remaining combined artillery would stay at the airport between the roads where they could support both groups. The Nineteenth Regiment's Second

Battalion would return from Yongdong and deploy along the Kap-ch'on River to block the western road. Its heavy mortar group, including Donnie's squad from Howe Company, would be deployed to the southwest of the city. The artillery would retreat from the airport to their position when required. The depleted Twenty-First Regiment would stay in reserve at Okch'on guarding that vital road to Yongdong to be used as the escape route. He ran out of troops before he could protect the southern route to Kumsan, so he released the reconnaissance company from their important primary duty of observing and reporting enemy movements to become infantry to protect that route. Though it provided more soldiers for defense, using the reconnaissance company as foot soldiers meant that they never provided any warning that the NKPA was already performing their now-standard envelopment maneuver in the south.

As they had done in all the previous battles, the NKPA Third and Fourth Divisions planned an envelopment attack for Taejon. When the rail bridge west of Taep'yong-ni was repaired, tanks and armored vehicles crossed in support of the infantry. The Fourth Division moved straight south and then came back to the east toward Taejon along all three of the major routes. The Third marched along the main rail line and formed the frontal attack. A major roadblock was then constructed on the escape route to the southeast on the road to Okch'on. Thus, all the major escape routes in and out of Taejon were blocked, and the horrible Americans were surrounded.

★ ★ ★

Kyu and his family did not know anything about the military's plans. They only knew that there had not been any trains on 18 July that took refugees. Early that evening, Sandara convinced them to return to the boarding house. They loaded the *sonsule* (handcart) and headed off, but when they got there, it was obviously abandoned. Sandara convinced them to return to her shop and apartment. At least there they could rest in peace and maybe clean up if the water was still running. So they set out on the thirty-minute walk from the boarding house to her shop. The streets were surprisingly quiet with few folks of any type about. A few refugees and a policeman or two were all that they saw.

When they were about ten minutes from the shop, suddenly two stooped *nongbu* (peasants) hobbled toward them. Kyu was immediately on guard as they were dressed suspiciously like his cousin at the rail station. When they got close, suddenly a third *nongbu* (peasant) jumped out from an alley. He was holding a rifle and told them not to move. The first two *nongbu* (peasants) came up to them, and Kyu immediately recognized his cousin. He wanted to embrace him, but his cousin waved him away. He asked if they had told anyone about seeing him at the train station. Kyu assured him that he saw no reason to tell anyone but his family here. That seemed to satisfy him. He then asked where they were going and why they left the train station. Kyu told them that there were no more trains expected until morning and that they were returning to the apartment of his wife's aunt. His cousin said that they could proceed but that they must be out of town by early tomorrow or suffer the consequences.

Though the electricity was off, the water was still running when Kyu and the weary travelers finally made it to Sandara's shop and apartment. The men took a quick bath, and then the women and child did, refreshing them all. Sandara went out into the courtyard behind the shop and scrounged some fresh vegetables, including cabbage, from the garden. Without any meat, the best that she could do was make *baechu doenjang guk* (cabbage and soybean paste soup) for dinner on the woodstove. It was warm and tasted delicious! The men had a *soju* (liquor) afterward and even Nabi had a small sip. They all fell asleep early, but not until after Kyu and Nabi enjoyed each other. Hopefully, tomorrow they would escape this dreadful city and head south.

19 JULY 1950,
TAEJON, KOREA

The NKPA attack on Taejon started in earnest early on the morning of 19 July. It began with their air force. Six Yak fighters struck the railroad bridge north of Okch'on. They also strafed the Twenty-First Regiment's headquarters near there and dropped surrender leaflets signed by GIs captured from Task Force Smith at Osan. Four other Yaks simultaneously strafed the Thirty-Fourth Infantry positions and the Taejon airport, two of which were shot down by antiaircraft fire. This was the last significant attack by the North Korean air force during the war. UN airpower concentrated on knocking out their air force and destroyed or damaged over forty-six NK planes that week. Thereafter, all enemy air attacks were of the Bedcheck Charlie–type where a single plane would fly over, drop one or two ineffective bombs, and scoot for home.

Most of the Nineteenth Regiment in Yongdong lost their vehicles at the roadblock at the Kum River. They did receive a few replacements from Pusan and confiscated additional but not enough to carry the entire battalion. So Colonel McGrail loaded the Second Battalion on a train and headed north early on the morning of 19 July. Donnie's Howe Company still had their Deuce and a Half, plus a number of jeeps and smaller trucks from their evacuation from the Kum River. Instead of taking the train, they drove the thirty miles north to Taejon and beat the rest of the battalion there by over an hour. They could hear cannon fire in the distance.

Donnie's thoughts were crowded as they waited for the train to arrive with the rest of the battalion: *I don't want to die. I am only eighteen years old. I've never married, never been treated as an adult. I never completed my education. I never had sex with the girl back home. I don't want to die, but I don't want to let my buddies down. I don't want to be judged yellow. As scared as I am, I don't have a choice. I must face the worst danger and try to be the type of soldier that I always dreamed I would be. I know I have lots of company.*[25]

The Second Battalion train made it to the Taejon rail yard about noon on Wednesday, 19 July. When they arrived, Colonel McGrail was informed that L Company of the Thirty-Fourth was under major attack near the Taejon airport, and he was ordered to rescue them. Colonel McGrail immediately marched E and F Companies abreast of each other north along the Nonsan Road to relieve L Company. Donnie, along with G and H Companies, was sent to occupy a hill about a mile to the south. The NKPA was attempting their standard envelopment maneuvers on L Company when E and F Companies arrived. Colonel McGrail found General Dean on-site directing the fire of two light tanks against the NKPA. Luckily, the companies of the Nineteenth were able to take the high ground before the NKPA and stopped the envelopment of L Company.

Donnie thought that the commands for more mortar shells would never end. His squad started delivering fire about 1330 and fired continuously until after 1600. They also received counter mortar fire back at them, the first time that he experienced someone firing in anger at him. But by 1700, the requests for mortar support slowed and then stopped. Donnie could still hear large volumes of rifle fire coming from the north where F Company was located. During the battle, the artillery of both armies duked it out with the airport taking quite a pounding. With the lull at 1700, Donnie could see the division's remaining artillery coming down the road from the airport headed toward the southwest corner of Taejon. It also looked like the Thirty-Fourth Command Post left the airport for downtown Taejon at the same time. The battle had been intense for Donnie while it lasted. Private Samuel Robertson was killed during the fight, and three others in Howe Company were wounded. That reduced the number of soldiers available for action in Howe Company to 131.

---

25   Colton, *Sacrificial Lambs*, 47.

About 1730, SFC Joseph Szito ordered Donnie's squad, the other 81 mm mortar crews, and the machine gun squads to mount into the jeeps and the Deuce and a Half truck. There were occasional rain showers during the evening from a typhoon that had just missed the area, so the roads were not dusty. They moved off toward the southwest of town as previously planned to set up near the rest of the artillery. They established temporary defensive positions and settled in for the evening with new C rations. WO Herbert Worzel recorded the day's activities in the morning reports as "moved by vehicle 30 miles North to Taejon where an attacked on the enemy (sic)."[26] Donnie got a few hours of rest until about 2200 when they heard what sounded like tanks off to the southwest. As the sound was coming from that direction, the NKPA must be performing an envelopment around the entire city. He figured that would be the end of sleep for a while.

Though General Dean was strategically in charge of the entire Nineteenth Division, Colonel Charles E. Beauchamp of the Thirty-Fourth Regiment was tactically in charge of the Battle of Taejon. Various battalion and company commanders recommended to him that they pull out the evening of 19 July, but Colonel Beauchamp felt that the division could hold on to Taejon for one more day and leave the afternoon of the twentieth. General Dean deferred to Colonel Beauchamp's decision. Other than the sounds of tanks and possible movements to the south, that evening was ominously quiet. Reports came into divisional headquarters of these movements and noises, and Colonel Beauchamp sent out a patrol to the south to check them out. They were never heard from again. Receiving no intelligence to the contrary and not knowing the danger, Colonel Beauchamp tragically stuck to his decision to stay in Taejon one more day.

---

26   H Company Nineteenth Infantry morning report dated 19 July 1950.

19 JULY 1950,
TAEJON, KOREA

The sounds of cannon fire and explosions woke Kyu up before dawn on Wednesday, 19 July. Though the explosions were not close, he could tell that the NKPA were shelling parts of the city. While picking the cabbage the previous evening, Sandara also gathered other vegetables, which she added to their meager supplies. After a last look around the apartment and the bare shop below, the refugees loaded the *sonsule* (handcart) and headed off to the train station. While walking, they could see smoke in a number of directions, but they didn't see any fire. They made it to the train station before 0800. It was still crowded with refugees. The ticket office was closed, and the status board was unchanged—northbound trains Canceled and southbound trains Delayed—so they sat down to wait.

The NKPA fired random cannon and mortar shells into the city starting early on the nineteenth. Mostly, these were to annoy and harass as they were infiltrating sharpshooters and other infantry into the city dressed as farmers to direct accurate fire later. However, the artillery duel with the US cannons located at the airport was very intense at times. They positioned their troops towards their standard envelopment maneuver of the entire city. With low clouds from the typhoon above, air attacks were impossible in the morning. The NKPA took advantage of the air force lull and transported tanks across the Kum River to start their advance on Taejon. They would use them that night.

While they were waiting, Kyu looked around at the other refugees. Most of the refugees appeared to be townsfolk from Taejon. He did not see any dressed as *nongbu* (peasants) like his cousin. He wasn't sure if that meant that the train station would now be a target or if they didn't need any additional intelligence about the incoming forces. Wounded soldiers started arriving about 1000. Hopefully, that implied that a train would be coming soon.

About noon, a long train with many passenger cars, boxcars, and flatbeds pulled into the station. It was Colonel McGrail's Second Battalion, Nineetenth Infantry, arriving back from Yongdong. There were a number of other army trucks pulled up outside the terminal, including the Deuce and a Half that Donnie Matney was on, but Kyu would never know that. Kyu had never seen a train empty so quickly. The army this time was in a hurry. They marched off from the train station within an hour, taking all their equipment and trucks with them.

There weren't that many wounded soldiers waiting to board the train. Maybe the army would let some of the refugees board this time? Kyu could hear what sounded like rifle and cannon fire coming from the direction of the airport. Both sounded pretty intense. The soldiers who vacated the train must have marched straight into battle. That would have been scary. But it also meant that the NKPA was getting close. They had better get onto this train!

Luckily, the morning clouds burned off, and the air force flew into the battle. They strafed and bombed a number of NKPA troop concentrations and knocked out five or six tanks in the early afternoon of 19 July. But the NKPA wasn't too concerned as most of their troops and tanks were camouflaged or under shelter by the time the skies cleared. They planned to attack that night when the air force didn't rule the skies.

Finally, an ROK official with an American officer, Captain Raymond D. Hatfield, stood up on the platform and started translating the announcements that the captain was making. Though it took a while for the crowd to be quiet, Kyu did hear that they would be taking refugees onto the train. Each had to have a day's worth of food and water. And they were loading only women and children for now. Nabi started to cry again. Kyu told her not to worry and to travel all the way to Pusan if he didn't get aboard. He would find her there somehow. Being practical, Aunt Sandara started dividing the food and supplies. The women couldn't take the *sonsule* (handcart), so the men would take the larger items in it while the women would take the smaller items, including some of the herbs and oils salvaged from the shop. Sandara said that she had friends in Pusan who owned a similar *yagcho silang* (herbal market) and they would either stay there or leave a message where they could be found. Kyu figured that there couldn't be that many *yagcho silang* (herbal markets) in Pusan and that would be a great way to meet later. Finally, all the belongings were split between the two groups, and the women said their goodbyes and started toward the train. Their final embrace was bittersweet. Sa-rang started to cry.

Kyu asked Him-chan whether they should just climb up on the boxcars and go along with the women and leave the cart behind. Him-chan said that might be pretty risky considering the attack on their original train when they arrived in Taejon. He said staying at the train terminal at least through the night should be safe enough in case another train pulled in, and then worst case, they would have to take off on foot over the mountains to the east of the rail yard later. So they settled down to wait. Though there was no additional food to be found, they were able to top off their water supply, including the *banhab* (canteens) that Nabi had left for Kyu.

A train did pull into the rail yard station later that afternoon. It had ten boxcars full of ammunition for both the ROK and the Americans. But before Captain Raymond Hatfield and the soldiers could stop them, the train engineer unhitched the engine and coal tender and started back down the tracks toward Yongdong. There was no way Kyu and Him-chan could ride in a boxcar to Pusan without a train engine to pull it.

That evening, Kyu and Him-chan stayed in the rail station. Kyu already missed Nabi and little Sa-rang. They ate some of the fresh vegetables that Sandara had gathered earlier because they knew that they wouldn't keep and would be heavy to carry if they had to walk out. Just as Kyu was finally falling asleep, a couple of shots rang out, and one of the soldiers guarding the rail station fell with a groan. The others quickly went into hiding positions, looking for a target to shoot. NKPA snipers had made it to the train station.

MORNING, **20 JULY 1950**, TAEJON, KOREA

The major NKPA attack against the Thirty-Fourth Infantry started around 0300 on 20 July. Tanks and infantry straddled both sides of the main road passing the airport while other troops attacked the right flank of the defensive position near there. Additional tanks passed beyond the Thirty-Fourth with at least six entering into town with infantry piled on top. The Thirty-Fourth's line commander telephoned Colonel Beauchamp that tanks had passed through his position and that they were under massive attack and would probably have to pull back. Colonel Beauchamp decided to drive out to see for himself. Just outside of town, a tank sprayed his jeep with machine gun fire, destroying it. Colonel Beauchamp was unhurt and crawled back to friendly lines where he convinced a 3.5-inch bazooka team to come with him. They were able to destroy the tank and capture the crew. This was the first successful 3.5-inch bazooka attack against a T-34 tank. The new bazooka used shaped ammunition charges designed by the Aberdeen Proving Ground that had only been in production for two weeks. The shaped charge was designed to explode on contact with the tank's armor with most of the explosion blowing into the tank causing massive amounts of shrapnel inside. It worked and was the first man-held weapon effective against the T-34. That same bazooka crew destroyed two more tanks later in the morning at the road intersection leading into Taejon. Colonel Beauchamp (code name Dragon) reported through the artillery stationed at the airport that tanks were in the area, but the Thirty-Fourth had the "situation well in hand."[27]

Colonel Beauchamp then ordered his reserve, the Thirty-Fourth Third Battalion to attack the gap between the Nineteenth and where the Thirty-Fourth First Regiment was supposed to be. They made little headway as they ran into six additional T-34 tanks and at least a battalion of NKPA. They withdrew back to their previous position with minor losses. Major Newton W. Lantron, their commander, left in a jeep to report what had happened and was never heard from again. Meanwhile, the Thirty-Fourth Infantry First Battalion was being unmercifully attacked and so started to pull back to the south company by company. Their withdrawal was not reported to Colonel Beauchamp as the telephone lines were cut and no radios functioned.

By 0400, the NKPA had occupied the airport and most of the positions north of town. They did not press their attack yet, waiting on other NKPA elements to get in position, most notably creating the roadblocks on the roads to the south of Taejon. But by 0800, they began attacking F Company of the Nineteenth.

As Donnie had surmised, sleep was fleeting for Howe Company that early morning of 20 July. It seemed that after 0300, they received another request for barrage or illumination rounds every fifteen to twenty minutes. There were rumors and false reports that part of the regiment had been overrun during the night. In truth, the only significant event was F Company being relocated two hundred yards south around daylight. By 0800, F Company was involved in a heavy firefight with the NKPA, and the requests for fire were constant. "We fired … till the barrels were red-hot, and everyone began to fire at the high ground in front of us."[28] Howe Company's 81 mm mortars supported F and the other companies of the Nineteenth until about 1030 when it became apparent that the companies were pulling back and fire would no longer be needed. Lieutenant Reagan ordered SFC Joseph Szito to pack the Deuce and a Half truck with the mortar and machine gun platoons and head into Taejon. At the main intersection, they passed three destroyed T-34 tanks and men from their sister G Company with bazookas manning a small roadblock. Colonel McGrail, seeing the size of the enemy attack, began pulling

---

27   Situation report from Captain Jessup, division artillery, 0750, 20 July.

28   Ent, *Fighting on the Brink: Defense of the Pusan Perimeter.*

the rest of Second Battalion south. He did not know at that time that the road into Taejon was still open and guarded by parts of G Company or that Howe Company had entered Taejon. By noon, all the Nineteenth Regiment Second Battalion's infantry had pulled out of their positions. Most were fleeing south through the mountains toward Kumsan and not toward Okch'on, where the Twenty-First was positioned in reserve. Only Howe Company; parts of G Company; and the kitchen, medical, and other support groups of the Nineteenth Second Battalion remained in Taejon proper.

The T-34 tanks that had passed the Thirty-Fourth Infantry earlier in the morning plodded into Taejon around daybreak and made it to the center of town where they off-loaded their infantry to act as sharpshooters and snipers. Two of the tanks then lumbered into the UN service area and promptly attacked about 150 soldiers in the area, blowing up vehicles and an ammunition truck and killing several. The tanks then rumbled off to attack other targets of opportunity, including two jeeps loaded with wounded outside of the Medical Company's headquarters and killing all but two. One tank rolled into the rail yard about midmorning, firing at supplies and equipment and starting a number of large fires.

Howe Company stopped not far from the divisional headquarters in town, and Lieutenant Reagan allowed the men to get grub or sack out. Never one to pass a chance for some shut-eye, Donnie joined SFC Joseph Szito and several others in a commandeered apartment overlooking the street leading to the divisional headquarters. Around 1300, they awoke to the sound of a tank lumbering down the road. It was an NKPA T-34. They ducked behind the window, and the tank just clanked by. That was as close to a tank as Donnie had been so far in Korea. It sure looked more powerful close-up than when observed from across the Kum River. A few minutes later, to Donnie's and SFC Joseph Szito's surprise, General Dean came bounding down the same street with a bazooka team in tow. "Which way did it go?[29]" he called out to SFC Joseph Szito, who pointed on down the street. General Dean, though strategically in charge, had left Colonel Beauchamp to handle the tactical details of the battle for the defense of Taejon. General Dean felt that his personal pursuit of tanks was calculated to inspire his men to become tank killers. General Dean and his personal

---

29   Hickey, *The Korean War: The West Confronts Communism.*

bazooka team did destroy at least two tanks that day. He would receive a Medal of Honor for his efforts.

After that, SFC Joseph Szito hiked to divisional headquarters to see what he could learn. He was surprised to see visitors, including the press, reviewing optimistic maps showing that all was well. They were even serving coffee. Not two blocks away, an NKPA tank sat in an alley, out of gas, with its crew outside smoking. With little experience in tank identification, members of the Twenty-Fourth Infantry passing by thought it was friendly. One US officer actually gave them ten gallons of gasoline, which they used to move the tank. Though there was the sound of occasional rifle fire and the rumble of a tank or two, Taejon in the early afternoon was eerily calm considering the forces that were then streaming together with the intent to annihilate each other. That would change drastically in the next few hours.

MORNING, **20 JULY 1950,**
TAEJON RAIL STATION,
KOREA

Kyu and Him-chan spent a restless night at the rail station. Starting about 0300, the continuous fire of rifles and cannons coming from the direction of the airport kept them awake, and snipers plucked away at any movement at the train station. About daybreak, they discussed whether to stay at the station to chance getting onto a train or flee using the road or climb into the hills. They decided that it would not hurt to ask the ROK translator what he knew. After a few minutes of searching while staying hidden from the snipers, they found him. He said that he expected one more train to come in to take the ten boxcars of ammunition back to Yongdong later that morning and that there would be a good chance for them to climb on top of it when it came. So Kyu and Him-chan decided to wait at the station until at least noon.

About 1000, much to their chagrin, an NKPA T-34 tank came clanking into the rail yard. It promptly opened fire at anything that moved using both its machine guns and main cannon. Numerous fires started and a couple of vehicles blew up. Luckily, it did not hit the ten cars full of ammunition, else the rail yard and part of the city would have ceased to exist. After what seemed like hours but was probably no more than ten or fifteen minutes, it clanked out of the rail yard toward a bridge across the Taejon River a couple thousand yards away.

About half an hour later, a shot-up train engine and tender pulled in. Kyu thought that this must be the engine that the translator expected. It hissed into the rail yard with steam escaping from multiple puncture wounds in the boiler. Captain Raymond Hatfield and the translator went out to meet it. There was much hand-waving and gesturing. After a few minutes, the captain and translator stomped off and the train engine turned around. There was no way that the damaged engine could pull the ten full boxcars back to Yongdong. So the engine started back toward Okch'on by itself. After traveling several miles, it was attacked by the NKPA with hand grenades and rifles before the first tunnel. The engineer was killed outright, and the fireman, though wounded, guided the damaged engine into Okch'on. Captain Raymond Hatfield called General Dean and told him that the ammunition boxcars were still at the train station. General Dean ordered Yongdong to send another engine to get them. After the shot-up engine left, Kyu and Him-chan decided that another exit route would be preferable to waiting for another train engine that may never make it through. They were correct. Captain Raymond Hatfield waited for that second engine to arrive there at the rail yard all day on 20 July. It never came. He disappeared and was never seen again. The ammunition cars were destroyed the next morning in a spectacular explosion by bombing by the USAF.

After filling their *banhab* (canteens) once more, Kyu and Him-chan started south out of the rail yard with all their remaining possessions piled in the *sonsule* (handcart). Their progress was slow. Once, they were fired at by snipers from the hills to the east, so they headed away from the exposed railroad and followed a parallel street in town. Kyu remembered the warning that his cousin had pronounced and hoped that they didn't run into him. They hoped that if they continued south, they would hit the main Okch'on road and be able to follow it. Taejon was now burning, and the smoke hurt their eyes. Up ahead, they saw a number of bands of soldiers that must be NKPA running with rifles into town. They hid and let them pass.

Going was slow. By late afternoon, they came to an underpass where the railroad crossed over the road. Suddenly a large line of US Army vehicles came cascading down the highway. All the soldiers onboard looked warily at Kyu and Him-chan but drove on past without stopping. Looking back toward where they came, Kyu could see additional army trucks continuing down a different road. It looked like they were being shot at by snipers in the buildings that weren't on fire. Him-chan stated that the road ahead was the road to Okch'on and the road to the left ended at a schoolyard against the mountains. They had to make a choice—go on farther through the fires and NKPA snipers along the Okch'on road or follow the trucks and hike out over the mountains from the schoolyard. They chose the latter.

AFTERNOON, **20 JULY 1950**, TAEJON, KOREA

After attacking and destroying the T-34, General Dean returned to the command post and ate a late lunch of heated C rations with Colonel Beauchamp. Both still believed that the situation was well in hand and the Thirty-Fourth and Nineteenth Regiments were deployed protecting the west side of Taejon. General Dean estimated that his forces were at 60 percent combat effectiveness, and morale was good according in his morning report to General Walker. With the weather improving, General Dean walked into the air coordination center and rattled their cages to get the air force flying to attack targets of opportunity, including the massed troops and tanks located out toward the airport. He also observed an attack against G Company at the crossroads and saw them hold their ground. Thinking that it was the entire Second Regiment of the Nineteenth and not just a few platoons, he felt that they were still in good shape but should consider withdrawing earlier than nightfall. He discussed this with Colonel Beauchamp, and the order to withdraw from Taejon was sent out about 1400. Colonel Beauchamp then left headquarters to scout the escape route.

Order to Open Okch'on road with tanks

Meanwhile, a truckful of mail was received at the command post from Yongdong with the driver reporting he had received sniper fire starting just outside of Taejon. A little later, a platoon of tanks arrived at headquarters from the First Cavalry Division's tank company. They joined with the medical group and a few other service groups and were the first convoy to move out toward Yongdong using the Okch'on road. Though they received sniper fire going through downtown Taejon, they had little trouble once out of the city and made it successfully through the tunnels and to the Twenty-First Infantry lines by about 1800. Colonel Beauchamp, who was checking this withdrawal route, saw the convoy pass by successfully and thought the route was clear. He also witnessed a train engine being attacked by rifles and grenades going through the nearby rail tunnels southbound. Instead of returning to the command post and running the battle as its commander, Colonel Beauchamp then drove south to the Twenty-First Regiment at Okch'on to ask why they were not guarding the tunnels and the withdrawal route. That order was never implemented, and to the dearth of the men still in Taejon, the road south to Okch'on and Yongdong was conceded to the NKPA. They would soon capitalize on this error and create a death trap.

Lieutenant Reagan and SFC Joseph Szito received the order to evacuate Taejon about 1500. They were informed that the remains of the Second Battalion of the Nineteenth Infantry, including Howe Company, would be the next to the last group out of the city. Donnie and the rest of the squad loaded the Deuce and a Half truck while others stood guard. Artillery and mortar shells began falling nearby and throughout the city. Several fires started, and the wooden buildings burst into flames like the kindling that they were made. No one tried to stop the fires, and soon blazes were raging on many streets. Snipers also fired randomly into the massed American soldiers. Warily watching the nearby windows, Donnie and the troops loaded the truck between chance rifle shots.

About that time, the artillery located at the southwest corner of town pulled out. The five remaining 155 mm howitzers drove toward town past the G Company roadblock. Seeing the artillery leave and the rest of the Nineteenth Infantry bug out, G Company finally left the roadblock and came into town. They were the last organized defense on the west side of town. The howitzers joined with other trucks in the next convoy and headed on through the city. The town was ablaze, and snipers were shooting from the windows of any building not on fire. The lead truck crashed into a tree and would not restart. The convoy then turned onto a side street to avoid the crash and was attacked by burp guns, mortars, and machine guns. All but one of the howitzers and all the ammunition were abandoned during that drive to get out of the city. The next convoy through would be sitting ducks for the NKPA.

General Dean returned to the command center and learned of the attacks and blocked roads going through the city. In the clear, he radioed the Nineteenth headquarters in Yongdong to send tanks north to help clear the roads. There are no records of this order ever being implemented. Since Beauchamp was absent, he then ordered the command post to tear down and prepare to withdraw. By this time, enemy mortar and artillery fire were hitting the entire city, including one hitting the latest medical section, wounding ten. More buildings caught fire. Smoke was everywhere. Taejon was starting to fall apart.

The final large convoy formed up at 1800 with G Company located in about the seventh or eighth truck from the front and Howe Company's Deuce and a Half truck third or fourth from the rear. Besides Lieutenant Reagan, among those known to be in the Howe

Company truck were SFC Joseph Szito, SFC David Scogin of the heavy machine gun platoon, PFC William Beitel, PFC Mike Marcin Jr., PFC Norman Warner, and PFC Donald Matney. General Dean expected that the convoy would take sniper fire while driving through Taejon but thought that they would be safe once they got outside of town on the road toward Okch'on as the Twenty-First should have had it well protected by then. He ordered that troops dismount and attack any snipers to keep the convoy moving through the streets of town. SFC David Scogin mounted a .30-caliber machine gun on the Howe Company truck, and SFC Joseph Szito made sure that the 60 mm and 81 mm mortars and ammunition were easily accessible. Donnie and the other soldiers on board also had rifles and ammunition. What a "police action"—the GIs were fleeing Taejon from the North Korean "bandits."

19th Infantry Troops withdraw from Taejon

★ ★ ★

Taejon was burning. To say the drive through it was hell would be an understatement. Burning debris fell on the streets. Buildings not burning contained NKPA machine gunners and snipers. Donnie and the troops were continuously firing and ducking as they encountered the enemy. "We were shooting from both sides of the truck as the driver wove his way through the streets."[30] The truck bounced over the rough road like a bucking bronco. Progress was slow. As drivers and trucks were shot up, the convoy diverted around them. A 2½-ton truck hit a building and almost blocked the entire main street. About fifty vehicles at the front of the convoy took a wrong turn under a railroad underpass and ended up bottlenecked in a schoolyard. With enemy fire coming in, these trucks were abandoned and almost 125 soldiers took off for the hills, including most of G Company. The rest of the convoy continued on through town along with the Deuce and a Half Howe Company truck. They reached a section of town where both sides of the street blazed like an inferno. Just beyond this point, General Dean's jeep missed the turn to Okch'on and enemy fire kept them from turning around. General Dean found himself in the same dead-end schoolyard as G Company and tried to hike out. He never made it.

The remainder of the last convoy continued on the Okch'on highway without its leader. But instead of being clear of the enemy and guarded by the Twenty-First, it found itself in a shooting gallery with the convoy as the target. The NKPA fired at them from both sides of the road. The road followed the railroad, and a small stream that made a U-shaped curve so that the convoy started to climb into the hills and headed back to the north. A mortar began lobbing shells at it, hitting the first truck and stopping the convoy's progress. A half-track came forward to push the truck out of the way, but its driver was shot and killed. About two miles out of Taejon, the convoy stalled under the intensive enemy fire coming mostly from the southeast side of the highway. The NKPA had created a one-and-a-half-mile gauntlet of bullets before the first tunnel that the convoy had just started to enter.

SFC Joseph Szito rallied Howe Company on the back of the Deuce and a Half truck. While SFC David Skogin fired cover using the truck-mounted machine gun, he had the platoon deploy a 60 mm mortar in a ditch. They fired twenty-four rounds of high explosives at the enemy on the south side of the road, but it didn't break up the NKPA attack. He then ordered Donnie and the rest of the heavy mortar squad to take cover in a ditch on the northwest side of the road. He directed Donnie's squad to set up the 81 mm and fire thirty

---

30   Ent, *Fighting on the Brink: Defense of the Pusan Perimeter*.

M57 WP (white phosphorous) rounds around the convoy to cloak the men in smoke so that the stalled vehicles in front could be pushed out of the way. While the smoke dissipated, he switched the 81 mm back to high explosives and dueled the enemy mortars. Though they were partially successful, the remaining NKPA mortars still scored direct hits on three additional vehicles near the end of the convoy, thus blocking both ends of the cavalcade. The enemy machine gun and mortar fire continued unabated even through the thick phosphorous smoke screen. SFC David Scogin moved the machine gun from the truck to the top of a hill on the north side of the road on an exposed rock and raked the enemy positions, but they still continued shooting. By 2045, with darkness setting in, an order was given to burn the vehicles in the convoy and take to the hills, every man for himself. Donnie and the rest of the company disabled the mortars as best as they could and took off up the side of the mountain.

Donnie Matney found himself with an M-1 rifle and a 1911 .45-caliber pistol on the west side of the hill below where SFC David Scogin had set up the machine gun. He was with others from his platoon and was beside PFC William Beitel. They were both scared. Bullets were flying in every direction. There was little cover, and they had to zigzag up the slope. Even though it was near sunset, it was still hot and sticky—over 90°F and 90 percent humidity. They had been in battle and under constant pressure for almost two days and under fire for over three hours that evening. Donnie had seen friends and other soldiers horrendously hurt and many died. The machine gun continued its *rata-tat-tat-tat*. Bullets zinged in all directions. Suddenly, PFC Mike Marcin cried out in pain nearby. He had been hit. PFC Theodore Brandow of the Thirty-Fourth Headquarters Company went over to help Marcin and was also hit. Nearby, PFC William Beitel also went down. Suddenly, Donnie felt a sharp pain in his abdomen. Looking down, he saw blood. He had been gutshot. Donnie's world went black.

AFTERNOON, **20 JULY 1950**, TAEJON, KOREA

Kyu and Him-chan passed the abandoned army trucks in the schoolyard. They could see about 125 soldiers climbing up the side of the mountain in groups of five to ten, mostly headed north to get away from the sounds of battle. They quickly unloaded what they could carry off the *sonsule* (handcart) and made simple *peuleim paeg* (A-frame packs) that they could carry. Whereas the soldiers seemed to be climbing north almost straight up the hillside, Him-chan convinced Kyu that they should climb at an easterly angle so that they could join the Okch'on road. That might put them closer to the battle, but they should have a better chance to escape. Kyu agreed.

★ ★ ★

As they wounded up the mountainside, the out-of-shape soldiers from the schoolyard clumped in several groups depending on how winded they were. The first group of at least thirty, after climbing for an hour and with darkness closing in, decided to stop and rest. They were never heard from again. The rest continued climbing north and then turned south after cresting a peak and traversing along the mountainside. Some made it to friendly lines the next morning. Some made it to safety by 22 July. Others just disappeared.

Kyu and Him-chan continued climbing the side of the mountain turning toward the southeast. They came to a saddle in the hills and followed it higher. Climbing through it at about dusk, they came to an overlook where they could see the Okch'on road to the south. It was covered with smoke from a long line of burning military vehicles of all shapes and sizes. With night falling quickly, they could make out NKPA soldiers climbing the hillside and kicking the fallen soldiers to see if they were still alive. Anyone who was alive and was able, they gathered as prisoners. The wounded, they shot in the head and did other atrocities to them.

Staying low, Kyu and Him-chan kept climbing over the hills, hopefully out of sight of the NKPA. Suddenly, they came upon a group of American soldiers who were resting. One of them shouted out and pointed a rifle at them. Kyu and Him-chan held up their hands. A man with an officer's uniform, Lieutenant Reagan, said nothing. SFC Joseph Szito said to search them and let them pass if clean. Lieutenant Reagan apparently abdicated his authority to SFC Joseph Szito to take command during the escape to get them to safety. After looking them over, they let them pass. Kyu and Him-chan continued hiking well into dark. They ate a light supper from the vegetables that the girls packed while they were hiking. The crescent moon gave them enough light to keep going for a while after sunset. They stopped for a short rest when it became too dark to travel and then restarted walking in the dawn's early glow. They forged a couple of streams and were able to use the A-frame packs as simple floats to get across another.

Traveling through the mountains and skirting the NKPA positions, Kyu and Him-chan finally made it to Okch'on by the afternoon of 21 July. After being searched and questioned by the Twenty-First Regiment roadblock, they were let go and even given a bit of cabbage. They continued on hiking to Yongdong and were able to climb on top of a boxcar of a casualty train that took them all the way to Pusan. There they found Nabi and the baby and Aunt Sandara without difficulty.

★ ★ ★

SFC Joseph Szito led the weary band of soldiers, including a subdued Lieutenant Reagan. They built a raft to carry the wounded across a rain-swollen stream and made it to safety on 22 July. They joined with the Nineteenth Infantry and Howe Company at Gimczon where the company was being reorganized and reequipped. The First Cavalry held the front lines now. Of the 144 in Howe Company who marched into battle, WO Herbert Worzel listed 71 men available for duty on 22 July. Forty-five names were itemized in the morning reports as either killed in action (KIA) or missing in action (MIA). Of these, seven were later identified as POWs. All seven of these died in captivity or were never repatriated. Donald E. Matney and nineteen others were not among the names recorded. Donnie was not listed in the morning reports as missing in action until a year later on 21 June 1951.[31]

---

31   Sweeney, *The Dead, the Missing, and the Captured*; Nineteenth Infantry, 41

SEYMOUR, MISSOURI,
OVER FIFTY YEARS LATER

The picture of the young man in the army service uniform with the ears sticking out graced the kitchen of my wife's mother all her life according to my wife, Sandy. That same picture was here in the kitchen of her Aunt Anna in Seymour, Missouri, where we were visiting in the early summer of 2002. Aunt Anna explained that it was a picture of her younger brother Donnie who had joined the army in 1949 at the tender age of seventeen and had never returned. He had been missing in action in Korea since July 1950. Oh, as the eldest remaining relative, she did receive a Christmas card every year from the president of the United States thanking her for his service. She also received various letters saying that they were still trying to find him and asking her to attend a briefing in Washington, DC, on what was being done to locate him. She and her sister Ruth who lived nearby even had their DNA taken so that it might help identify Donnie's remains someday. But nothing had ever really happened—nothing since Aunt Anna had requested that the army provide compensation and a headstone to place in the Seymour cemetery in Donnie's memory next to their mother, Willa, back in 1988.

Cpl Donald Matney

Willa passed away in 1965 at the age of sixty-nine without ever knowing what truly happened to Donnie. She did receive a telegram in late July 1950 notifying her that Donnie was missing in action. As she had not yet received Donnie's letter saying that he was going to Korea, the telegram was how she learned that he was no longer in Japan. She was quite shocked by the telegram and did not know what to do. She received a follow-up letter dated 28 August 1950 from Major General Edward Witsell, adjutant general of the army, explaining that PFC Donald E. Matney had been reported missing in action in Korea since 20 July 1950. He explained that *missing in action* (MIA) was used to indicate that the whereabouts or status of an individual is not immediately known. He further stated that every effort would be exerted continuously to clear up the status of such personnel, but under battle conditions, that was a difficult task. Often persons identified as MIA during battle would be reported as returned to duty or hospitalized for injuries. He also noted that Donnie's pay and benefits would continue until his status was resolved. Willa was heartbroken. She had only allowed Donnie to join the army as it was peacetime, and he would get a chance to satisfy some of his wanderlust. She never thought that he could just disappear.

A year later, Willa received a letter from the Army Effects Bureau dated 10 October 1951 asking her if she would mind keeping Donnie's personal items until his MIA status was resolved. Included with the letter was a form listing those items as a billfold, springs, bundle of photographs, a Japanese hat emblem, box of fish hooks, a stamper with pad, a belt, a box of letters and papers, a skate key, two New Testaments, a Bible, a key ring, and miscellaneous citations, ribbons, and brass. Willa agreed and had them sent to her home in Seymour, Missouri.

abm/cll

AGPO-CO 201 Matney, Donald E.   28 August 1950
(19 Aug 50) 231041

Mrs. Willa M. Matney
Seymour, Missouri

Dear Mrs. Matney:

    I regret that I must confirm my recent telegram in which you were informed that your son, Private First Class Donald E. Matney, RA 17273184, Infantry, has been reported missing in action in Korea since 20 July 1950.

    I know that added distress is caused by failure to receive more information or details. Therefore, I wish to assure you that at any time additional information is received it will be transmitted to you without delay.

    The term "missing in action" is used only to indicate that the whereabouts or status of an individual is not immediately known. It is not intended to convey the impression that the case is closed. I wish to emphasize that every effort is exerted continuously to clear up the status of our personnel. Under battle conditions this is a difficult task as you must readily realize. Experience has shown that many persons reported missing in action are subsequently reported as returned to duty or being hospitalized for injuries.

    In order to relieve financial worry on the part of the dependents of military personnel being carried in a missing in action status, Congress enacted legislation which continues the pay, allowances and allotments of such persons until their status is definitely established.

    Permit me to extend to you my heartfelt sympathy during this period of uncertainty.

                Sincerely yours,

                EDWARD F. WITSELL
                Major General, USA
                The Adjutant General of the Army

1 Inclosure
Bulletin of Information

Letter Confirming MIA Status

★ ★ ★

Aunt Anna pulled out her old photo album. She had a few precious pictures or mementos of Donnie. The personal items that Willa had received had disappeared long ago. Sandy's mom had none, so we made copies of what Anna had so that she could have pictures as well. There was a picture of Willa with Donnie, his older sister, Maxine, and younger brother, Leonard, taken in about 1940 outside their old home. There was another taken in about 1947 or 1948 with Anna and her husband, Jay. And then there was the one taken when Sandy's mom was visiting with Sandy's older brothers before Sandy was born. Donnie's older brother Billy was also there. It had to have been taken just before Donnie joined the army in 1949. He was leaning on his side on the ground with the others, hat cocked jauntily, silly grin, and sticky-out ears, and all. That was the sum total of the physical mementos that remained of Donnie's life.

We did all the things families do when visiting—eating and laughing a lot, visiting Matney Hollow and the old cemetery, and seeing the few other changes that occurred in the small whistle-stop town of Seymour, Missouri. We didn't think much more about Uncle Donnie for eight more years. By then, both Sandy's mom and Aunt Annie had passed away, and Aunt Ruth was now the matriarch of the family. She called one day in June 2010 to tell us that she had received a letter from the government asking her if she wanted to attend an update on the investigation status to locate Uncle Donnie. She could not attend and wondered if we would like to go. She sent us the letter.

The letter was from the deputy assistant secretary of defense inviting Aunt Ruth as the official next of kin and one other to attend a briefing at the Sheraton Tysons Hotel at Tysons Corners in Vienna, Virginia. The briefing would provide an update on the progress that various sections of the Department of Defense had made to resolve outstanding MIA (missing in action) and POW (prisoner of war) cases from the Korean conflict and Cold War. She could also request a specific update on Uncle Donnie if she contacted his appropriate case officer within the army. The letter stated that she could delegate who would attend and that whoever did attend would be flown in coach from their nearest major airport to Washington, DC, at no cost, but travel to and from the hotel to the airport, room, and board would not be included. We jumped at the chance to get a free flight to visit our nation's capital.

Sandy and I had no idea what we were attending. We flew coach from Denver to Dulles Airport and rented a car. We showed up the next morning for the free conference not knowing what to expect. Having no concept of the war in Korea, we learned that the first three months of the Korean conflict were considered the most violent in recorded history. The NKPA were experienced warriors from the civil war battles in China and with the Japanese during WWII. They were dedicated to conquering all of Korea within three weeks. They had no regard for the Geneva Convention and knew no rules of war. Captured soldiers almost always died, sometimes by gruesome torture. The NKPA had the highest prisoner-of-war death rate ever recorded. The odds on Uncle Donnie being alive were very, very slim. Finding his remains would be like finding a needle in a haystack.

But there were hundreds of others attending the conference hoping that a miracle might occur and the fate of their loved ones would be discovered. For two days, we listened as different officials from the Department of Defense described their group's efforts to recover and identify unknown remains from the Korean War. They talked about the hope of DNA analysis. They talked about trying to get into North Korea to help identify lost graves of GIs. They talked about the efforts to identify the remains in the 208 coffins provided by North Korea during the 1990s. Parts of over 450 GIs were thought to be among those remains with only 181 identified so far, and many of these were not American. They talked about the previous visits to North Korea between 1996 and 2005 where thirty-three sites were excavated recovering 229 sets of remains. They talked about the 866 remains of unknown soldiers buried in the Punchbowl in Hawaii. It was an emotional rollercoaster. People cried. Some yelled. Most just sat back and shook their heads.

We were overwhelmed that first year. They did give us a folder with general information about the war and Uncle Donnie. It included a two-page broad summary of the Twenty-Fourth Infantry Division activities leading up to the battle at Taejon. It stated that Uncle Donnie disappeared there and no one knew when or how. It said that they had done exhaustive interviews and searches for him, but no clue to his whereabouts had ever been found. We went home saddened and confused.

AUGUST 1950, KOREA

After the fall of Taejon, the remains of the Twenty-Fourth Infantry Division retreated to Yongdong to its previously built defensive positions and later dropped back farther south to Masan. It had lost its commanding general and suffered 30 percent casualties. More than 2,400 men were missing in action. During its two and a half weeks of battle, this understrength division held the advancement of the two top divisions of the NKPA to six miles per day. It had done its job delaying the enemy's attack, but it was exhausted. Help was on the way. During their delaying tactics, General Walker transported the rest of the Eighth Army to Pusan. First to take up positions against the NKPA and relieve the Twenty-Fourth Infantry was the First Cavalry. They fought hard but still could not stop the NKPA's advance. Chuck Farr, Donnie's friend from Seymour who rode the train with him to Basic, lost his life on 23 July fighting for the First Cavalry just south of Taejon three days after Donnie disappeared. The marines landed. They fought to keep the NKPA from taking Pusan from the east. Then the Second Infantry Division and the Twenty-Fifth Infantry Division arrived. They had time to dig secure defensive positions around Pusan without immediate NKPA attacks. The US had successfully traded land for time to bring in more troops. Finally, sufficient troops landed to stop the continued thrusts of the NKPA. The tempo of the war changed from fight and retreat to stand and fight.

The Pusan Perimeter was established by 4 August 1950. The Pusan Perimeter encompassed an area approximately one hundred miles north to south and fifty miles east to west. The Naktong River bound it to the west, the Sea of Japan to the east, and forbidding mountains to the north. The sacrifices of the Twenty-Fourth Infantry and overwhelming airpower crushed the NKPA armor and provided the time needed to construct the Pusan Perimeter. Battles fought prior to its establishment were won by the NKPA using tanks and their inevitable infantry envelopment maneuver. Once the perimeter was created, known friendly forces manned each side of the UN defensive positions with a reserve force readily available to stop any breakthrough. The NKPA tactic of an end run around the sides of an emplacement no longer worked, and anti-tank weapons arrived countering their armor. The effect on improving morale and the willingness to fight by the US forces cannot be overstated.

Oh, the NKPA tried valiantly to break this defensive line. They attacked much of the perimeter simultaneously and were pushed back. They attacked one area in depth but were stopped. They attacked again and again. Each time they were repulsed. Both SFC Joseph Szito and Lieutenant Reagan survived Taejon and rebuilt Howe Company as part of the Pusan defenses. They fought in many battles behind the Pusan Perimeter, including the ten-day First Battle of the Naktong Bulge against their nemesis, the NKPA Fourth Division. Sure, Lieutenant Reagan was still insecure. Many battles and months of soldiering elapsed before he became a respected leader. He was finally promoted to captain and received a Silver Star for gallantry by leading a small squad to recapture Howe Company's heavy mortars taken by the NKPA in November 1950. He stayed in the army after the war and was promoted to major in 1954. He died in 1979 in Fayetteville, Arkansas. SFC Joseph Szito voiced criticism of the early war efforts and has been quoted by many authors in numerous books. He was field promoted to second lieutenant at the Battle for Chinu and briefly commanded F Company there but reverted to master sergeant when he retired from the army after the war. He died in Monterey, California, in 1993.

★ ★ ★

Other than the occasional *Stars and Stripes*[32] newspaper, external information for the frontline troops inside the Pusan Perimeter was limited to the radio station hosted by Seoul City Sue. Broadcasted from a captured radio in Seoul, she spouted NKPA

---

32   *Stars and Stripes* military newspaper was first published on 9 November 1861.

propaganda, played popular American music, and provided the occasional news story slanted to North Korean views. She constantly harangued the soldiers to surrender immediately or be punished severely beyond comprehension. Most of the Americans laughed at her words when gathered together but became melancholic and nostalgic when listening to her music when alone.

While the NKPA attacked the Pusan Perimeter, the air force continued to bomb both strategically and tactically. They blew up bridges and factories in the north. They attacked freight trains traveling south. They bombed convoys and single trucks. The flood of men and materials needed by the NKPA to fight dried up to a mere trickle. The NKPA resorted to drafting any able person they could capture and forced them to be shock troops during an attack. They were given no weapons and were told to pick one up off the dead on the battlefield. If they did not attack, they were shot from behind. Food also became scarce, and many NKPA troops lived on one meal a day, if that, as the days fighting on the Pusan Perimeter wore on.

An estimated 380,000 refugees like Kyu and Nabi crowded into the UN-held territory during two weeks in the middle of July. That number increased by 25,000 daily through July. Almost a million refugees crowded inside the Pusan Perimeter once it was established. The city of Pusan was especially crowded, and clean water was a scarcity. Water vendors carrying two large buckets made from used oil drums walking the streets was a common sight. Food was also a challenge. Scavenging the edible discards from US bases, refugees created something they called UN stew, but more often called *kkulkkuli chuk* (pigs' soup). People made money however they could— gathering driftwood for fires, selling water, or scrounging discarded materials for temporary housing. Petty theft and prostitution were common. Nevertheless, schools still functioned with classrooms often open-air and attended by over one hundred students per class. Violent crime and gangs were present but were never a serious threat. Outside the cities, the refugees were pushed to the southwestern parts of the country where the rice fields were located to minimize impacts to the military. General Church banned all civilians within five miles of the perimeter battle area under threat of immediate execution. He hoped to stop the flood of refugees from influencing the army's ability to fight. He was only partially successful.

The ROK Army rebuilt its manpower from these refugees. Kyu joined the fighting First Division, survived the war, and left the army the equivalent of a staff sergeant. The ROK First Division became the only ROK unit to operate as part of the US Eighth Army I Corps. Its commander, Colonel Paik Sun-yup, later was promoted as the first Korean four-star general. Him-chan became an ROK intelligence officer and retired in the late 1960s from the ROK equivalent of the CIA. He did marry Sandara after the war. Both Sandara and Nabi volunteered as nurses during the war, though Nabi took a few months off in 1951 to give birth to their first son. From the low point of about fifty thousand soldiers after the fall of Seoul, the ROK fielded more than eighty-two thousand soldiers for the defense of the Pusan Perimeter.

All these new soldiers would be needed as the NKPA launched an all-out assault from the northeast against the Pusan Perimeter around the Naktong River in their final attempt to drive the UN and the Americans into the sea. Starting at the end of August, they fought for fifteen straight days with the battle lines ebbing and flowing back and forth from five points along the perimeter. In what was called the Great Naktong Offensive, the NKPA launched major attacks against the cities of Taegu, Masan, Kyongju, Yongch'on, and across the Naktong Bulge. Sometimes they made headway, but the UN forces were always able to rally and rush in reinforcements to recapture the ground lost. By then, the UN forces were numerically superior, technologically further advanced, and better supplied. After two weeks, the NKPA attack stalled out. This was to be the NKPA's final push to throw the ROK and its allies into the sea. General MacArthur completed his strategy to stop the NKPA once and for all and planned to drive them out of South Korea.

SEPTEMBER 2011

S andy and I attended our second Korea / Cold War Annual Government Briefing at the beginning of September 2011. This time, we were a bit better prepared. We requested a briefing from the army's assigned casualty officer. We also signed up for the tour of the Pentagon's POW/MIA corridor. Again, we traveled for free from DIA (Denver International Airport) to Dulles using the government's COIN Assist program through Carlson Wagonlit Travel. We rented a car at Dulles and stayed at the Sheraton Premier at Tyson's Corner where the update was to be held. This time, we took notice of the many displays and booths set up outside the venue. Many different groups support the MIA/POW families. Some had pictures and photos from the war. Others helped link relatives with members from the same regiments or companies to share information. And of course, each of the involved defense department commands had self-promotion stations and information on what they did.

At this time, the Defense Prisoner of War/Missing Personnel Office (DPMO) was the main organization coordinating these events. Located in Crystal City, Virginia, it oversaw the efforts to locate, account for, and repatriate captured and missing Americans as a result of hostile actions. DPMO's stated purpose was to provide the expertise, technology, and resources needed to perform this mission with integrity and dedication. We first met William "Shorty" Cox, who then worked for DPMO, at their table at this conference.

The Joint POW/MIA Accounting Command (JPAC) was a joint force within the Department of Defense tasked with accounting for all missing and listed military POWs from past conflicts. Its headquarters was located at Hickam Air Force Base in Hawaii. It included the Central Identification Laboratory where remains were examined for identification purposes. It oversaw three foreign-based commands in Thailand, Vietnam, and Laos who coordinated remains' recovery. JPAC handled four main areas—analysis and investigation, recovery, identification, and closure.

The Armed Forces DNA Identification Laboratory (AFDIL) located in Rockville, Maryland, was recognized as the world leader in the analysis of DNA. The mitochondrial (mtDNA) section supported the Central Identification Lab in Hawaii with the identification of service remains.

Other groups that supported and were represented at the conference included the Department of Veterans Affairs (DVA), the Library of Congress (LOC), the National Personnel Records Center (NPRC), the American Battle Monuments Commission (ABMC), and Arlington National Cemetery.

Each of these agencies and others gave updates during the conference. Keynote speakers included USAF major general Craig A. Franklin, the vice director, Joint Chiefs of Staff, the Pentagon, and sergeant major of the army Raymond F. Chandler. Robert J. Newberry, the deputy assistant secretary of defense, in charge of DPAC, hosted the conference.

The AFDIL presentation on how DNA is used to forensically identify remains was the best speech that year. According to it, there are three types of DNA found in cells of the body that can be used for identification purposes. Nuclear or autosomal DNA are the twenty-three chromosomes unique to each individual and can be found in almost every human cell. It stays the same throughout life and can be obtained from the smallest viable biological sample. Since 1992, over 6.1 million service members have provided a direct reference specimen to be used to identify remains from combat or training operations. The second type of DNA is the Y DNA found only on the twenty-third chromosome of all males. It is useful when adequate direct references or parent-sibling references are not available to perform nuclear DNA testing. The third type of DNA is mitochondrial DNA (mtDNA). Whereas the other two types of DNA degrade fairly rapidly over time, mtDNA in teeth and bones can last for thousands of years. It is passed hereditably through the mother's lineage and stays the same for dozens of generations. MtDNA analysis is used to help identify many recovered remains.

Using the polymerase chain reaction process, scientists can amplify the mtDNA in the smallest biological sample for analysis. Once amplified, the sample is then mapped out into the individual components using a process called sequencing. Once sequenced, the mtDNA can then be compared to existing known maternal relative samples. Unluckily, mtDNA is not exact as it does not change for dozens of generations. Persons thought to be unrelated may actually have a common ancestor many generations removed and thus have the same mtDNA. It is best used to reduce the number of potential candidates. Sandy was so taken by the DNA presentation given by AFDIL that she went over to their booth afterward and had her DNA sampled.

We met with the army's assigned casualty officer Sergeant Emma Walker for Uncle Donnie's case. She provided us with the standard two-page blurb common to the thousands of Twenty-Fourth Infantry Division casualties lost at Taejon and the Kum River. It basically said the Twenty-Fourth Infantry Division fought a series of battles between Osan and Taejon and the army doesn't know what happened to Uncle Donnie. They continue to look for him but have no new evidence. We didn't expect much, but the report was pathetic. We asked her to research three things for us—identify Donnie's role in the army, tell us where he was last seen, and provide us with the company's daily reports from the start of the war through July 1950. We didn't know if this information would help us, but we had to try something.

That evening, large buses took us to the Pentagon to view the POW/MIA corridor and the outside Pentagon Memorial. They hustled us through security and into the vastness that was the world's largest building during the 1940s and 1950s. We boarded elevators to the third floor where the hallway was lined with information and stories about POWs and MIAs from many conflicts. We listened to a short presentation and then were given time to wander through the displays listing the stories and mementos from those lost and missing in action. Dedicated the previous fall on 15 September 2010, the corridor reminded us that America is one of only a handful of countries that care to repatriate fallen soldiers. We then went outside to see the Pentagon Memorial where American Airlines Flight 77 cratered.

The conference the next day was more of the same. We sat at round tables and, between presentations, shared stories with other families about their missing relatives. At that time, 8,195 servicemen were listed as missing in action in Korea of the 36,923 who gave their lives in the cause of liberty for others. We heard presentations on research and analysis, archival research, research methodology, and the challenges in scientific identification. Again, we were awed. We were fascinated. We felt pride and also sadness. But the final takeaway from that year's conference was that from 2005 through 2009, JPAC disinterred 7 remains from the Korean War and was successful in identifying only 6. From 1982, despite spending millions of dollars, the remains of only 246 out of some 8,441 Korean War POW/MIAs were positively identified—less than eight per year. It might take a very long time to identify Uncle Donnie.

SEPTEMBER 1950, KOREA

Under the code name Chromite, through shear stubbornness and willfulness, General MacArthur landed the marines at Inchon just southwest of Seoul on 15 September 1950. The navy opposed landing there due to the area's treacherous high tides. The Joint Chiefs of Staff opposed it due to their belief that Inchon would be heavily defended. But General MacArthur persevered and launched a second offensive front to recapture Seoul and split the NKPA forces in the south away from their supply lines in the north. To the surprise of the Joint Chiefs, the landing at Inchon happened virtually unopposed. The port was secured quickly, and the troops marched inland. Within two weeks, by 28 September, just ninety days after the NKPA captured it, Seoul was liberated, and the supply lines to the NKPA army in the south severed completely.

The next day, a jubilant General MacArthur, President Rhee, and various other ROK dignitaries flew into Kimpo Airfield and paraded into Seoul to wildly cheering throngs of freed South Koreans lining the streets. Promptly at noon, MacArthur strode to the dais in the damaged National Assembly Hall where he said, "Mr. President, by the grace of a merciful providence, our forces fighting under the standard of that greatest hope and inspiration of mankind, the United Nations, have liberated this ancient capital city of Korea. In behalf of the United Nations Command, I am happy to restore to you, Mr. President, the seat of your government that from it you may better fulfill your constitutional responsibilities."[33] All but overcome with

---

33 Appleman, *South to the Naktong, North to the Yalu*, 537.

emotion, President Rhee responded, "How can I ever explain to you my own undying gratitude and that of the Korean people?"[34] President Truman later messaged MacArthur: "Few operations in military history can match either the delaying action where you traded space for time in which to build up your forces, or the brilliant maneuver which has now resulted in the liberation of Seoul."[35]

The capture of Seoul was a rout. Of the greater than thirty thousand NKPA troops deployed to protect Seoul and Yongdungp'o, over seven thousand were taken prisoner and fourteen thousand killed. At least forty-five tanks were destroyed and significant artillery and ammunitions captured, including twenty tons of untouched US ammunition stashed in a warehouse before the fall of Seoul in June. UN loss numbered about three thousand five hundred casualties with less than seven hundred of these resulting in death.

Once the Inchon invasion was underway, the orders to the troops within the Pusan Perimeter were to "break out of the Pusan Perimeter, then pursue and destroy the North Koreans at all points as rapidly as possible."[36] All three regiments of the Twenty-Fourth Infantry Division headed north from the Naktong River on the road toward Taejon, leapfrogging each other to keep the pressure on the NKPA. The NKPA pulled back but established roadblocks along the way starting at Kumch'on. It became clear that these battles were delaying actions to provide time for the NKPA soldiers to retreat northward and destroy what they couldn't take with them. But with their supply lines severed, the NKPA battalions fell below 50 percent in strength, were low on ammunition, and lacked fuel. By 26 September, after defeating the delaying action at Kumch'on, the Nineteenth Infantry arrived back at Yongdong. There they liberated three Americans held prisoner in the local jail. They proceeded to Okch'on, ten miles east of Taejon, where another NKPA delaying force defended the road and railway tunnels to provide time for the thousands of their soldiers still in Taejon to escape. This force held the division in place for a day but melted away during the night of 27 September. The Nineteenth Infantry then marched from Okch'on on the highway toward Taejon past the rusting hulks of the vehicles

34 Appleman, *South to the Naktong, North to the Yalu*, 537.

35 Appleman, *South to the Naktong, North to the Yalu*, 537.

36 Weiler, *Korean War Odyssey a.k.a. World War Three*, 24.

destroyed at the NKPA roadblock where Donnie Matney disappeared nine weeks prior. Along the way, they picked up two Americans who had hidden out in the hills the entire time the NKPA were there. Lieutenant Reagan and SFC Joseph Szito reentered Taejon with the Nineteenth Regiment around 1600 on 28 September.

Taejon was a burnt fragment of the city it once was. Between the NKPA and the air force, most buildings were damaged or destroyed. But the worst was yet to be discovered. After the NKPA captured Taejon, they gathered the civilians who had not fled their advance. Those whom they could not conscript as soldiers or as comforters and whom they viewed as enemies, they piled into the city jail and the Catholic mission. At least eight thousand civilians were thus imprisoned. They also housed about sixty Americans and fifty ROK prisoners in the city jail. When the Pusan Perimeter breakout occurred, the NKPA started taking the civilian prisoners out in groups of one hundred—the old, men, women, and children included—and shot them with captured American M1 rifles using armor-piercing ammo. They fell dead into the surrounding American-dug defensive slit trenches and were covered by a thin layer of dirt. They then did the same to the ROK and American prisoners in the city jail. Up to seven thousand civilians were killed this way in the Taejon Massacre. One American, Sergeant Carey H. Weinel, survived and later testified to Congress about the event. Though he was shot three times and buried alive, after seven or eight hours of effort, he was able to wiggle his head free and yell for help. Another American who survived being shot and buried alive died within a couple of days. One ROK soldier and three civilians also survived. Another American, Sergeant Ralph L. Kilpatrick, who disappeared from the Nineteenth Regiment's C Company at the Kum River on 13 July came into town forty-five pounds lighter having survived the NKPA invasion by eating melons and raiding vegetable gardens.

The number of NKPA prisoners captured around and inside Taejon numbered in the thousands. Few supplies made it to the NKPA through the blockade from the Inchon landing. Without food, ammunition, or fuel, many NKPA gave up for the promise of a hot meal. Though some were South Koreans pressed into service, many others were hard-core NKPA who surrendered. Most of these were interrogated by second-generation American Japanese nisei as Japanese was often the only common language understood due to the prior war. One of the most important of those captured was Sr. Col. Lee Hak Ku, the NKPA Thirteenth Division's chief of staff who walked to US lines and awoke two sleeping guards of the Eighth Cavalry. He became the highest ranking NKPA captured up to that time. These prisoners were all treated with respect per the Geneva Conventions.

The same was not true for the prisoners taken by the NKPA. Seven hundred fifty-eight American POWs held by the fleeing NKPA were forced to march north on foot with little food by a brutal NKPA officer known as Tiger. Many had no shoes. Those unable to walk were clubbed or shot and left by the roadside dead. They stopped at the Moo Hak girl's school in Seoul where the last names of approximately 300 POWs were recorded. They then continued the march north into the far reaches of North Korea. Of the original 758, only 262 survived the brutal Tiger Death March all the way from Taejon and the Pusan Perimeter to the Apex POW Camps near the Yalu River that separates North Korea from Manchuria. The rest perished, and few have been identified since.

POW "Tiger March"

An additional 350 American prisoners were in Seoul when the Inchon landing occurred. The NKPA loaded them into boxcars so solidly that they could not sit and sent them north by rail to P'yongyang, the capital of North Korea. Twenty were able to escape. With no food or water, 30 died en route and only 300 were alive in the train when they arrived. By mid-October, with the UN forces in hot pursuit, the train headed north again, leaving P'yongyang on 18 October. Ten more miraculously escaped. The train stopped two days later at Sunchon Tunnel where exactly 100 men were taken off the last car of the train, supposedly to get food. The train left. Instead of food, the prisoners were shot in cold blood, and the guards fled.

Seventy-five died, but amazingly, 25 wounded and emancipated soldiers survived and were rescued by the First Cavalry. The train continued north to the Kujang Tunnel, where the track ahead was destroyed. There again, about 33 were gunned down and, amazingly, 3 survived. The remaining 125 were marched north from there with 122 of them disappearing forever, most killed by violence from the guards. The 3 remaining joined up with the Tiger Death March group and were marched to the Apex Camps south of the Yalu River. Only two survived the war.

The treatment of prisoners by the Reds was dismal the first eighteen months of the war. Starvation and indoctrination into the virtues of communism were their fate. Fully 43 percent of those captured died in captivity. POWs had a choice of becoming cooperative (progressive) and receiving more food or being resistive (reactionary) and suffering starvation, beatings, and torture. Approximately 25 percent of US POWs became progressive, including thirty-six airmen who "confessed" that the US used germ warfare against the NKPA. This poor treatment continued until December 1951 when the communists provided their first list of POW names. Once names were confirmed, the communists decided to increase food supplies as explaining the high death rates would be counterproductive. Their indoctrination attempts did continue as they hoped that returning POWs would remain susceptible to communist influence after the war when at home.

All the UN divisions pushed the NKPA northward from the Pusan Perimeter. By the end of September, the Inchon landing troops linked up with the advance at Osan and reached to Seoul. Provisions to the NKPA faltered. The decimated NKPA retreated above the 38th parallel as fast as their limited supply of fuel and the relentless bombing and attacks would allow.

SEPTEMBER 2013

Sandy received a letter dated 28 September 2011 from the Armed Forces Medical Examiner System confirming that they had received her DNA sample. It further stated that the sample would only be used if remains were found that might be her uncle Donnie and then only for comparison purposes if DNA could be extracted from those remains. It said that it could take up to a year to sequence her DNA but she could request a copy of the final results. Of course, Sandy requested a copy.

&lm

AGR8-N 201 Matney, Donald E.   31 December 1953
RA 17 273 184 (31 Dec 53)

Mrs. Willa M. Matney

Seymour, Missouri

Dear Mrs. Matney:

    Since your son, Corporal Donald E. Matney, RA 17 273 184, Infantry, was reported missing in action on 20 July 1950, the Department of the Army has entertained the hope that he survived and that information would be received dispelling the uncertainty surrounding his absence. However, as in many cases, no information has been received to clarify his status.

    Full consideration has been given to all information bearing on the absence, including all records, reports and circumstances. These have been carefully reviewed and considered. In view of the lapse of time without information to support a continued presumption of survival the Department of the Army must terminate such absence by a presumptive finding of death. Accordingly, an official finding of death has been recorded under the provisions of Public Law 490, 77th Congress, approved March 7, 1942, as amended.

    The finding does not establish an actual or probable date of death. However, as required by law it includes a presumptive date of death for the termination of pay and allowances, settlement of accounts and payment of death gratuities. In this case this date has been set as 31 December 1953.

    I regret the necessity for this message but hope that the ending of a long period of uncertainty may give at least some small measure of consolation. I trust that you may find sustaining comfort in the realization that your loved one made the supreme sacrifice while serving honorably in our country's cause.

                        Sincerely yours,

2 Inclosures   WM. E. BERGIN
  DA Pamphlet No. 20-15   Major General, USA
  Copy Finding of Death   The Adjutant General
  (In duplicate)

Willa Informed Donnie Presumed Dead

We also received a letter and a package dated 27 March 2012 from Maj. Jorge A. Rosario, our army casualty liaison officer, who confirmed that Corporal Donald Matney was assigned to H Company of the Nineteenth Infantry Regiment, Twenty-Fourth Infantry Division, as part of a four-man 81 mm heavy mortar crew. He also provided a CD with copies of H Company's morning reports from mid-June through July 1950 and other documents discovered pertaining to Uncle Donnie. The morning reports were previously classified and had been declassified in the past few years. Even so, quite a few events and names were redacted, especially in the late part of June 1950 while H Company was still located in Japan.

Company morning reports are cryptic documents created each day to report important statistics and changes at the company level. They tell of all personnel updates and movements at a company level. From them, we learned of the major events that occurred to H Company from the start of the war in mid-June through the end of July 1950. Donald Matney's company was one of the last of the Nineteenth Infantry Regiment to arrive in Korea by sea from Japan and was deployed to the East Coast to protect the airport at Yonil. They saw their first action at the Kum River and were one of only two fighting companies of the Nineteenth that retreated through Taejon. Except for the medical and support groups, the remaining companies evacuated with the Second Battalion to the south toward Kumsan. Though most of his compatriots that were lost at Taejon were listed in the morning reports, surprisingly, Donald Matney was not listed on any of the supplied pages. We learned later from other sources[37] that Donald Matney was not reported as missing in action in the morning reports until a year later on 21 June 1951.

The other documents our casualty officer included were quite sparse. They encompassed notices that Donald Matney was listed as MIA at the Punchbowl memorial in Hawaii, a copy of the letter notifying Willa that he was declared MIA, his death notice in December 1953, and his personal effects list of items that were sent to Willa. Other important information concerning his service with the army was destroyed in the fire at the National Personnel Records Center (NPRC) in St. Louis, Missouri.

The NPRC held the responsibility for maintaining the service records for all army personnel discharged from 1 November 1912 through 1 January 1960 and all air force personnel discharged from 25 September 1947 through 1 January 1964. The fire began after midnight on 12 July 1973, and firefighters were on-site within five minutes after the alarm was raised. The fire started on the

---

37   Sweeney, *The Dead, the Missing, and the Captured*; Nineteenth Infantry, 41.

sixth floor and was so intense that the firefighters were forced to withdraw from the building by 0315. It burned out of control for over twenty-two hours and was not fully extinguished for over two days. It took the participation of forty-two fire districts to fight the fire, and the damage was so severe no root cause was ever identified. As no cross-references, copies, or microfiche existed of the mass of paper records, losses can only be estimated at between fourteen and sixteen million records destroyed. Miraculously, neither the flames nor the tremendous amounts of water used to put them out hurt the microfiche reels of the army and air force morning reports located on a lower floor. An additional six million records were waterlogged and sent to McDonnell Douglas and NASA, where they were restored using a vacuum-drying process designed for the Mercury space program. Donnie's basic service and September through December 1949 training records were destroyed in the fire, but his limited medical records, service in Korea, and the company morning reports survived.

The 2013 Korea / Cold War Annual Government Briefing was held at the Hyatt Regency Crystal City in Arlington, Virginia, at the end of August. Armed with the daily reports, Sandy and I felt for sure that we would make headway in discovering what had happened to Uncle Donnie. As in previous years, over 250 attended. We met with Shorty Cox briefly and also met with our army casualty officer, a new lady. We requested any additional information that might be available. They also reported that a second identification lab had been setup at Offutt AFB (air force base) outside of Omaha to help speed up the identification of remains.

That year's presentations included one on how remains were handled during the early part of the war when Uncle Donnie disappeared. During the first six months of the war, each active army division established temporary cemeteries to hold their fallen soldiers. The Twenty-Fourth Infantry Division set up Cemetery No. 1 in Taejon by 9 July 1950. Finally, a combined United Nations cemetery was established in Tanggok, outside of Pusan, on 6 April 1951. The American Graves Registration Services (AGRS) then began the tedious task of exhuming all the temporary cemeteries and moving all the bodies to Tanggok. Those that were properly identified were shipped back to the US or formally interred based on the desires of the deceased's relatives. Much effort went into rectifying those that could not be identified, but if still unknown, the remains were shipped to the army's Central Identification Unit (CIU) in Kukora, Japan, for further processing. If still unidentifiable, the remains were treated with a 48–50 percent formaldehyde solution for three to five days for preservation. In 1956, 848 unknown remains were moved from Kukora, Japan, to the National Memorial Cemetery of the Pacific in the Punchbowl near Honolulu, Hawaii. An additional 19 remains were added to the Punchbowl during the next fifteen years, and one set of remains was randomly selected and moved to Arlington as the official unknown soldier for the Korean War.

The 2013 field trip was to Arlington National Cemetery, where we visited the Tomb of the Unknown Soldier and witnessed the changing of the guard. Arlington was established during the Civil War on lands seized from the plantation of Confederate general Robert E. Lee. It sits on a hillside above the Potomac River with a grand view of downtown Washington, DC. The Tomb of the Unknown Soldier is near the top of the hillside. A large white marble sarcophagus is located above the original grave of the soldier buried there from World War I on Veteran's Day, 11 November 1921. The east side of the sarcophagus facing Washington, DC, is carved with three Greek figures representing peace, victory, and valor. Crypts of unknowns from World War II, Korea, and Vietnam (now empty) lie to the west and are marked with white marble slabs. The monument is guarded twenty-four hours a day seven days a week by a sentinel from the Old Guard, or the Third Infantry Regiment, founded in 1784 and the longest-serving active duty infantry unit in the US Army. Each guard must have a perfect uniform and perform a choreographed march of twenty-one steps with an armed rifle on his shoulder. It is grueling work and takes a special soldier to be selected as a sentinel. Less than 10 percent of those who apply are chosen. It typically takes eight hours for a sentinel to prepare his uniform before his rotation. Each rotation is one hour long during the winter and half an hour long during the summer. Each sentinel is on duty for twenty-four hours straight along with three others and a relief commander. The tomb has been continuously guarded that way, rain or shine, since 1937.

We also learned during the seminar about the many lists that have been compiled of the men captured by the NKPA. One of the most famous was compiled by Sergeant Wayne "Johnnie" Johnson, a scout for L Company, Twenty-First Regiment, who was captured in early

July 1950 at Choch'iwon. He recorded and memorized 496 names of other POWs that he met or was told about from other POWs during the long Tiger Death March to the north and during his stay at the Apex POW Camp. This list is often referenced and is considered very accurate. We also learned that last names of prisoners were written on chalkboards when POWs were housed in schools and churches during transport. Though usually only last names, these chalk board lists provide evidence for POWs captured early in the war. After the war, returning POWs were debriefed and relayed whom they saw and remembered from their stay at the camps. And after the fall of the USSR, the archives of the KGB and Kremlin were opened for a short while and researchers were able to locate POW lists from the Korean War that the Soviets received. These also included names of a couple of Americans who were captured and relocated to the Soviet Union. Matney was not a name that we could find on any of these lists. So it was unlikely that the young mortar man with the ears that stuck out was ever recorded as a prisoner of war of the NKPA, Chinese, or Russians.

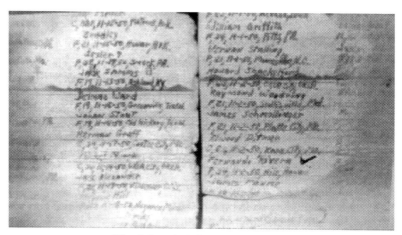

The Johnnie Johnson POW List

On the afternoon of the second day, we met John Zimmerlee for the first time in the hotel atrium. John Zimmerlee is an author, the inventor of the Stream Dancer and VersaBoat, and an investigative historian. John's father, Captain John H. Zimmerlee Jr., was a bombardier on a B-26B bomber of the 730th Bomber Squad. His father's plane disappeared the night of 22 March 1952 on a mission near Kangdong, North Korea, when he was just two. His father's remains have never been identified, and John now dedicates a large portion of his life to goading the US government into identifying the remains of unknowns from the Korean War. For over twenty years, John has built up databases incorporating information on thousands of POW and MIA personnel from the Korean and Cold War era. Through a number of Freedom of Information requests, John has forced the government to declassify information kept secret for over sixty years. He and his wife, Melissa, have spent hundreds of hours photocopying microfiche and paper records in the National Archives released by these requests. Often requests for declassification, mandatory by law, would go unanswered and have to be resubmitted. But slowly, painfully, John has built up an impressive list cross-referencing MIA and POW information from all sorts of sources. He unearthed a list of 944 unrepatriated American POWs that the US government knew about after the war when the list was declassified in 2009. Television reporters and newspapers worldwide often quote John.

Through his research, John is convinced that the reason that the Korean War is referred to as the Forgotten War is because the US government told every returning soldier not to talk about it. The government told them that talking may endanger those still missing. While men were being slaughtered in the battle zones, a large number were also being captured, and the Chinese would publish these names in their newspapers. The *New York Times* would translate these articles and reprint the thousands of names of POWs. That made it appear to the public that the UN was losing. The government had to do something to keep morale high at home. So according to John, they started a practice to label soldiers as either KIA or MIA or anything but POW unless they were forced to do so because the names were published as having been captured. Time after time he discovered information from his Freedom of Information requests that would show that the government had information that a soldier was captured by the NKPA but they still listed them officially as MIA or KIA.

John gets personal about his search for information about his father. His research discovered references to a 1961 report suggesting the B-26 gunner on his father's plane had been captured. When he first requested a copy of that document from JPAC, they claimed that they didn't know where to find it. When he sent them the document reference number, they replied with a letter that the document didn't exist. The next week, John himself found the document easily at the National Archives.

When we met John, there was a line of three or four others in front of us seeking information on their loved ones. At that time, John had just published *American Trophies: How US POWs Were Surrendered to North Korea, China, and Russia by Washington's "Cynical Attitude"* with Mark Sauter. It is an investigative summary of their joint discoveries on how Russia, China, and the North Koreans continue to play the US government on the search for Korean War POWs/MIAs. We talked with John for fifteen or twenty minutes about Donald Matney and what we had learned about him. We promised to e-mail him the morning reports that we had received, and he promised to send us any information on him that he might have in his extensive files.

SEPTEMBER–OCTOBER 1950, KOREA

The charge continued in the race to retake South Korea
and kick the NKPA out. By late September, the NKPA was
reduced to mere shells of its original strength and was fleeing
headlong back into North Korea. Traveling mostly on foot, the ROK
Capital, Sixth and Eighth Divisions pursued the NKPA relentlessly,
often traveling faster and farther than the mechanized US forces.
"Too little has been said in praise of the South Korean army which
has performed so magnificently in helping turn this war from the
defensive to the offensive,"[38] said General Walker of the Eighth Army
to the *New York Times* on 25 September 1950. By 30 September, the
ROK Third Division was only five miles south of the 38th parallel on
the eastern costal road to Kangnung, the farthest north of any UN
command.

The amount of NKPA equipment destroyed and abandoned
during this mad rush back North is truly astounding. T-34 tanks
destroyed and abandoned numbered 239, and no known tanks made it
North. Seventy-four self-propelled 76 mm guns were also destroyed.
Over 12,700 NKPA soldiers surrendered, including 200 who laid
down their arms when requested by a Mosquito spotter plane dropping
a note from the air with no ground support personnel nearby. Best
estimates are that no more than 30,000 NKPA escaped South Korea to
North Korea to fight again. Many others were purified by the North

---

38   Appleman, *South to the Naktong, North to the Yalu*, 599.

Korean political police as advancing UN soldiers found numerous unarmed NKPA gunned down in cold blood by their own.

On 27 September, General MacArthur received authorization to proceed north of the 38th parallel to destroy the North Korean armed services. He was to reunite all of Korea under Syngman Rhee if possible and to report immediately if Soviet or Chinese intervention appeared imminent. Under no circumstances should any UN forces cross into Chinese or Soviet territory. Both the Chinese and the Soviets issued stern warnings that any foreign aggression wantonly invading North Korea would not be tolerated. On 1 October, General MacArthur issued a demand to the commander in chief of the NKPA to lay down arms and cease hostilities. There was no response. On 9 October, General MacArthur issued an ultimatum demanding their complete surrender. The following morning, Premier Kim Il-Sung in a radio announcement from P'yongyang, rejected that offer. North Korea would not surrender.

The ROK Army then launched its advance across the 38th parallel into North Korea. The ROK Capital and Third Divisions captured the important port city of Wonsan on the east coast by 11 October. Within a week, the Capital Division marched north fifty miles and captured the harbor of Hungnam, thus depriving the NKPA resupply by sea from these important ports. Prior, General MacArthur scheduled the marines to land at Wonsan to be part of a four-part pincher to capture the North Korean capital of P'yongyang. He expected their landing to be much easier now that the port itself was in control of the ROK.

The First ROK and the US First Cavalry began pushing into North Korea on 9 October with the First Cavalry attacking from Kaesŏng on the west side and the First ROK charging from their old stomping grounds at Korangp'o-ri to the east. Kyu with the First Division was within a few miles of his homestead as the ROK battled their way north. They met the US Fifth Cavalry late in the afternoon of 12 October. By 14 October, the three defensive lines the enemy developed to protect the North Korean capital city of P'yongyang collapsed, and the NKPA was in utter disarray. Four major UN thrusts steadily moved forward to seize this ancient city, the oldest in Korea, with the Fifth Cavalry designated to be the first to capture it. When the Fifth Cavalry discovered the Taedong River bridges into downtown were destroyed, they were stymied entering the city from the south. However, General Paik Sun-yup[39] of the ROK First Division grew up in P'yongyang, so he, with the ROK First, crossed using a river ford he knew from his childhood a couple of miles west. By evening of 19 October, Kyu and the ROK First were well entrenched in downtown P'yongyang. The ROK Seventh Division entered from the east while the American Fifth Cavalry sat without a way to cross the Taedong River to the south. By 1000 the next day, the ROK First Division declared the city secure, including the city hall, the provincial government offices, and the NK People's Committee offices. And on 24 October, Bob Hope, Marilyn Maxwell, and Les Brown and His Band of Renown entertained the troops outside of P'yongyang. Meanwhile, the marines, the fourth prong of the planned attack, sat stuck in ships outside of Wonsan ninety-one miles away waiting for the harbor to be cleared of mines while the ROK Third Division jeered at them from shore.

The UN forces continued marching northward. By 24 October, the ROK First and Sixth Divisions made it to thirty miles of mainland China and the Yalu River. The US Twenty-Fourth Division with now Captain Reagan and First Lieutenant Joseph Szito marched north of P'yongyang and started its push for the border and the Yalu River. Near the small town of Anju on 5 November, Captain Reagan earned a Silver Star recovering the heavy mortars and other equipment captured by the NKPA. And the marines, as part of XX Corps, started their march northward toward destiny at the Chosin Reservoir. However, logistics for all these men and equipment were stretched thin—the rail lines stopped over two hundred miles south and the treacherous roads were often mined and pockmarked by bombs. Trucks operated around the clock trying to supply the frontline troops but with few spare parts for the unavoidable needed repairs. Airdrops were made when possible, but most frontline troops operated with less than twenty-four hours of supplies on hand. Though the NKPA appeared beaten, the UN forces were stretched close to the breaking point. On 27 October, General MacArthur rescinded the limits on UN forces other than the ROK to stay below thirty miles from the Yalu and ordered them to pursue the NKPA up to the edges of the NK border. The Joint Chiefs of Staff cautioned General MacArthur that this countermanded their directive of 27 September, but he

---

39 General Paik Sun-yup became the ROK's first four-star general at the age of thirty-two.

replied that it was a necessity of the war and had been approved by President Truman at their meeting on Wake Island.

Most of the soldiers thought the war would be over by Christmas. General MacArthur went so far as to cancel inbound shipments of ammunition from America and stopped additional troop replacements. He activated the Civil Assistance Command on 30 October, tasked with helping the ROK transition to civilian life. He felt that the war would end soon. The Twenty-Fourth Division made it to within spitting distance of the Yalu River with some of its patrols reportedly crossing its frozen surface into China. Even with the supply lines spread so thin, General MacArthur flew in hot turkey dinners with dressing, mashed potatoes, and pumpkin pie for Thanksgiving for everyone on the front lines. He felt it was time to celebrate.

But then the Chinese intervened.

EARLY 2014

In our search for answers to what happened to Uncle
Donnie, I expanded my research in 2014 and started locating
additional books and websites about the Korean War. I found
a number of great resources, including a PDF copy of the 1949
Nineteenth Infantry Regiment yearbook[40] from their time at Camp
Chickamauga in Beppu, Kyushu, Japan. Though printed four months
before Uncle Donnie joined the Nineteenth Regiment, it did provide
meaningful background on his time spent there and pictures of the
men that served with him. I also located many firsthand accounts
from veterans who had been at the Kum River and Taejon. One of
my favorites was a clip from a war history video series put out by the
army called *The Big Picture*, episode "TV 169—The First 40 Days
in Korea" downloadable from the National Archives and through
Youtube.com. It details the beginning of the war and has many scenes
taken during the battles at Taejon and the Kum River. Apparently
narrated by Humphrey Bogart, the episode shows the fighting during
that last day as the convoy tried to leave Taejon. Though we could
not identify him, it is possible that Uncle Donnie was one of the
doughboys[41] riding in the back of a Deuce and a Half truck fighting its
way through the streets of this Korean city. Pictures in many history

---

40   *The Organization Day Yearbook of the Nineteenth United States Infantry
     Regiment*, September 20, 1949.

41   According to *24th Forward*, *doughboy* was a word-symbol for Nineteenth
     Infantry command and vehicles. Likewise, *Danger Forward* identified the
     Twenty-Fourth Infantry Division headquarters.

books on the Battle of Taejon are extracted from this original army footage.

Surprisingly, the key events that occurred to H Company Nineteenth Infantry during this early part of the war are chronicled in a number of books. They tally very close to the sparse narrative provided by the H Company daily reports. Lieutenant Reagan is mentioned, though his name is spelled differently in places. SFC Joseph Szito is quoted often and is quite outspoken. I didn't put it together that he was Uncle Donnie's squad leader until much later, but he is listed in numerous places as in charge of the 81 mm mortar section of H Company. The Deuce and a Half truck assigned to the company is even mentioned. All of this background information helped us to partially understand what Uncle Donnie went through and to feel closer to finding him.

We received John Zimmerlee's analysis of Uncle Donnie's case early in 2014. He confirmed that he could not find any reference to Donald Matney in his extensive files and matrices of prisoners of war taken by the NKPA, Chinese, and Russians. He felt that it was more likely that Donald Matney had been killed in action. He did identify two X-files that the Department of Defense and the American Graves Registration Service (AGRS) associated as possibly being Corporal Matney. The X-files, unlike the TV series about aliens, were the case numbers given to remains that the AGRS deemed unidentifiable. Most of them are now buried in the Punchbowl National Cemetery outside of Honolulu, Hawaii.

Unknown X-900 was recovered from a shallow grave near the crest of a hill two hundred yards west of the village of Kwangjong-ni near the main rail line off Route No. 1 about eleven miles north of Kongju where the Thirty-Fourth Regiment defended the Kum River. The remains were of a male Caucasian, twenty to twenty-three in age, brownish hair, and about $5'9\frac{5}{8}''$ in height. Cotton drawers and fatigue trousers were found with the remains with multiple laundry marks, one of which could have been Donald Matney's. The skeleton was mostly complete and contained all its teeth. The original report, dated 14 April 1951, stated that death most likely occurred in July 1950. The report noted that the remains had a healed fracture of the right radius and a healed fracture of the right ulna distal third. Though we didn't think Uncle Donnie had broken either of these bones while at home, it was possible that it happened later in the army. Included in the files were review identification reports dated 27 March 1953, 5 November 1953, 10 September 1954, and 13 February 1956. The September 1954 indicated that 274 unknown remains could be associated with X-900, but 25 were most likely. Donald Matney was number twenty-one on that list.

We didn't think X-900 felt right for Uncle Donnie. First off, he was shorter at 5'8" versus the $5'9^5/_8$" of the remains, and he was younger. He also didn't have any known healed fractures. His hair was more copper or red color, and the reported remains were brown. He was also reported in Taejon, and though it was possible for him to travel north above Kongju, more than likely he would have tried to head south. But why we really decided X-900 could not be him was the report collected by the AGRS from the civilian Noh Jaesung on 4 April 1951 who claimed to have buried these remains. He stated in Korean that he buried X-900 on 12 July 1950. We knew from the morning reports that Uncle Donnie was in transit north from Yonil on that date. We felt that there was little chance that X-900 was him.

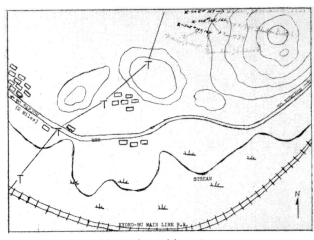

X-739 burial location

Unknown X-739 was recovered from a common grave on the side of a hill with unknown X-740 on 19 March 1951 a quarter of a mile north of the main Taejon-Okch'on supply route and about two miles east of Taejon near the beginning of the location of the NKPA major roadblock set up to stop the retreat from Taejon. The remains were of a male Caucasian, seventeen to nineteen in age, and about 5'8½" in height. Cotton drawers were found with the remains with laundry mark *M-318?* and a web cartridge pouch with two illegible markings. Also found with the remains were a web belt, pistol belt, jacket, canteen with cover and cup, and a first-aid pouch. The skeleton was mostly complete and contained most of its teeth. The remains showed evidence of wounds in the left femur, pelvic region, and head. The left leg, hands, and most of the bones from the feet were missing.

Farmer Chung In Tek was interviewed on 19 March 1951 and stated that townsmen made a number of burials around his farm and that he buried two in a joint grave when he was plowing his field after the battle on 20 July 1950. AGRS search and recovery operation no. 165 performed by the 565th Graves Registration Company, Sergeant Robert Savidge leading, recovered remains X-739 and X-740 from a common grave at that location on that same March date after the interview. Three other remains were recovered nearby—Mike Marcin and Norman Warner from H Company Nineteenth Infantry and Theodore Brandow, HQ Company, Thirty-Fourth Infantry.

The preliminary report on X-739, completed 25 March 1951, concluded that identification was not possible without additional dental records. A processing report created at Tanggok on 7 August 1951 reiterated the same findings. A secondary identification report was created a year later on 24 March 1952 that indicated that 50 open MIA reports were compared to X-739. It noted that X-740, found in the same grave, had been identified as belonging to William Beitel, H Company Nineteenth Infantry, missing since 20 July 1950. It concluded that without additional dental records, the X-739 remains were unidentifiable. A third report was written in Kukora, Japan, on 27 September 1954. This report included infrared pictures of the laundry markings and noted that they were consistent with four casualties that had already been identified and returned home and two MIAs—Sergeant Enoch Montoya and possibly Corporal Donald Matney. It further noted that 397 open MIA cases were compared to the remains. A final report was created in Kukora, Japan, on 10 October 1954 stating that the remains could also be that of Corporal John C. Morris III, E Company Nineteenth Infantry, based on height and dental records. A separate burial statement from Mr. Su Sung Yong stated that he had buried two remains in a common grave near where X-739 was found later on 10 August 1950. X-739 and X-740 could have been these remains. Nonetheless, Corporal Morris was first reported missing in action 31 July 1950. After his repatriation in

1953, Corporal Carl N. Anderson noted him as a POW still in NKPA hands. But without additional dental records, the remains would have to remain as unidentifiable. On 10 February 1956, X-739 was shipped from Kukora, Japan, to the Punchbowl in Hawaii for final burial as an unknown.

X-739 Laundry Marks

We really thought hard and prayed about X-739. Back in the 1950s, the army believed it most likely to be one of three soldiers—Sergeant Enoch Montoya, Corporal John C. Morris, and Corporal Donald E. Matney. Sergeant Montoya disappeared on 2 November 1950 while these remains were buried no later than 10 August 1950. He was 5'5" tall while the remains were most likely 5'8½" tall. He was twenty years old while the remains were most likely seventeen to nineteen years old. Corporal John C. Morris disappeared 31 July 1950 from Chinju, farther south, but could have wandered back to Taejon and been buried on 10 August. How he could have ended up in a common grave with Corporal Beitel who disappeared 20 July cannot easily be explained. He was 5'10" tall while the remains were 5'8½". He also was twenty years old when he went missing, but the remains were most likely seventeen to nineteen years old. However, his dental records most closely matched those of X-739. Corporal Donald E. Matney disappeared on 20 July, the same date death occurred for X-739 as stated by Chung In Tek in his burial report. He was 5'8" in height, close to the best estimate height of X-739. He was eighteen years old when he disappeared, between the best guess ages of seventeen to nineteen for X-739. He was also in H Company, the same as Corporal Beitel, the identified remains buried in the same grave. However, Donnie's only known dental record was a simple manual chart of teeth taken in August 1949 when he entered the army during basic training. It was handwritten and did not match the remains, but who knew how accurate this manual charting was?

We also received another data package from our army casualty officer. This package included printouts on the searches for Corporal Matney as well as additional correspondence that was in the file. The army started field search case (FSC) 16-F right after the recapture of Taejon in late September 1950. All the missing-in-action personnel from Taejon and the Kum River, including Corporal Donald Matney, were included in this search list. No firm evidence was ever located for him. A detailed search specifically for him was performed in October 1950 with no luck. A second search was conducted by the AGRS on 25 June through 24 July 1952 for all the open cases on FSC 16-F. This search was conducted throughout the outskirts of Taejon, including the Thirty-Fourth's headquarters, the southern exit route, and the roadblock to the tunnel on the Okch'on road. No additional graves were located. Interviews conducted later in the war suggested that Corporal Matney may have left Taejon on the southern road with Corporal Joe Madril and the other companies of the Nineteenth Infantry Second Battalion instead of staying in town with the rest of H Company and taking the Okch'on road with the convoy at the end. There were lots of theories and possibilities for what happened to Uncle Donnie but nothing concrete in the supplied files.

AGPS-GC 201 Matney, Donald E.   19 May 1954
RA 17 273 184 (10 May 54)

Mrs. Willa M. Matney

Seymour, Missouri

Dear Mrs. Matney:

In the letter dated 31 December 1953 you were informed that an
official presumptive finding of death has been recorded for your son,
Corporal Donald E. Matney, RA 17 273 184, with date of death set as
31 December 1953.

This office and the Far East Command are exhausting every effort
in an attempt to resolve our Korean casualties. It is, therefore, of
vital importance that our files contain all available dental and physical
data pertaining to the individual casualties.

The files of our military personnel contain a record of any dental
treatment received and any bone fractures sustained during their military service, however, there is a possibility that your son may have
received treatment by a civilian dentist which is not reflected in his
Army records. It will be of vast assistance in our efforts to complete
Donald's file if you can furnish any dental or physical information recorded by your family dentist or doctor for your son prior to his entry
into military service and any other information concerning outstanding
dental or physical characteristics such as fractures, malformed bones,
and peculiarities in the dentition of the teeth. Any X-rays of bones
or teeth which your son may have had made will also aid us in our investigation.

An envelope addressed to the Office of The Quartermaster General
is inclosed for your convenience in replying. If you prefer to forward
the name and address of Donald's dentist and/or doctor, the Office of
The Quartermaster General will gladly contact him for any information
which he may have.

                                    Sincerely yours,

1 Incl   JOHN A. KLEIN
Envelope (TQMG)   Major General, USA
                                    Acting The Adjutant General
OTQMG
IDENTIFICATION BRANCH:
ATTN: Miss Martin, Rm 2539 "B"

Army Requests Donnie's Dental Records

Included with the other correspondence were letters concerning
Donnie's dental records. The first letter, dated 19 May 1954 from
Major General John A. Klein, asked Willa Matney, Donnie's mother,
to provide contact information on Donald Matney's dentist. She
replied with a handwritten letter on 13 July 1954 that Donald never
had any dental work done in his hometown of Seymour, Missouri,

but he had x-rays and a tooth extracted in Colby, Kansas, by a dentist named Dr. Parrot. When contacted, Dr. Parrot responded that he had no record of treating Donald Matney but that there were two other dentists in Colby and maybe one of them had. The army then contacted Dr. C. R. Storer in Colby, who responded he had not seen or treated Donald Matney. The third dentist, Dr. B. H. Arnold, responded in September 1954 to a second request with a handwritten note that he had indeed removed the lower left first molar of Donald Matney on 15 March 1946 and had taken x-rays. Unluckily, the x-rays had been destroyed in an office fire. The army was unable to obtain any additional dental records on Donald Matney and thus had no way to compare them against X-739. So X-739 was declared unknown in October 1954.

We were convinced that X-739 was Sandy's uncle, Donald Matney. On 25 April 2014, we sent an e-mail to William "Shorty" Cox at DPMO with a carbon copy to John Zimmerlee outlining our findings and officially requesting that X-739 be exhumed for identification.

NOVEMBER 1950 THROUGH MARCH 1951, KOREA

Though signs that the Chinese Communist Party (CCP) army infiltrated North Korea existed as early as the end of October, General MacArthur still believed that they would not intercede. In reality, almost 450,000 CCP troops deployed along the Yalu River by 25 September and at least three of these divisions crossed into North Korea. A telegram from Stalin to Mao dated 5 July 1950 stated this: "We think it correct to concentrate nine Chinese division on the Chinese-Korean border for volunteer operations in North Korea in the event the enemy crosses the 38th parallel. We will try to provide the air cover of these units."[42] Even though they attacked and practically destroyed the ROK II Corps in late October, General MacArthur believed that these were NKPA and Chinese volunteers as they had melted back into the mountains and had not been seen since. So on 24 November, the day after feeding the frontline troops a hot Thanksgiving dinner with all the trimmings, General MacArthur announced final victory would be achieved through a Christmas push to the Yalu River. The next day, the CCP Army launched a two-pronged attack—one to the east against the marines and X Corps at the Chosin Reservoir and one to the west against the remainder of the UN forces.

---

42 Telegram 5 July 1950 from Stalin and Molotov to Mao and Zhou through Flippov.

On the east side, the battle at the Chosin Reservoir was particularly intense. Significantly outnumbered, the marines and X Corps maintained strict military discipline and escaped through contested mountain roads and valleys with the majority of their forces intact. One marine commander quipped, "We're not retreating—we're just advancing in a different direction."[43] They retreated to the port city of Hungnam on 11 December and withdrew by 24 December after destroying anything usable in that port city. Noteworthy during the withdrawal, the SS *Meredith Victory,* designed to hold twelve crew and no passengers, successfully sailed with fourteen thousand refugees on board standing shoulder-to-shoulder for three days through a minefield, enemy shelling, and bitter cold to arrive safely to the island of Koje-Do in the south. In all, over 190 shiploads of men, materials, and supplies evacuated from Hungnam back to Pusan in order to bolster the flagging Eighth Army and help stop the CCP onslaught.

On the west side of North Korea, the Nineteenth Infantry, with the British Twenty-Seventh Brigade to the west and the ROK First Division to the east, guarded the strategic Ch'ongch'on River bridgehead. Against many savage attacks, they held this location to buy time for the UN forces to withdraw. Additional countries had joined the ROK and Americans in the fight. The British Twenty-Seventh Brigade took part in the earlier capture of P'yongyang, along with the Third Battalion, Royal Australian Regiment. The British marched in perfect cadence in flashy kilts with bony knees sticking out and a bagpiper leading the way. When attacked, they had a reputation of holding the line and staying in place until they ran out of ammunition and then retreating under control. They were assigned to work with the Twenty-Fourth Division, and Tommy and the Taro Leaf soldiers got along merrily. Thailand sent the Thai Expeditionary Force. The French Battalion arrived, and the Netherlands Detachment, a battalion, came into the fight. Out of the ten thousand planned, a battalion of Canadians arrived in early November. None of these forces could stand up to the onslaught of the CCP Army led by the Mongolian herd on horseback armed with broad swords and burp guns. But then came the Turks.

Most feared by the North Koreans was the Turkish Brigade who arrived in Korea in early October 1950. Usually bearded and armed

---

43 This quote is attributed to the famous Major General Oliver P. Smith, commander of First Marine Division.

with both a rifle and a large broad sword, it was said that a Turk would cut off an opponent's head before they could draw their weapon. The Turks also had a penchant for taking trophies from their defeated enemies. Many a Turk wore a necklace made of the ears, noses, and fingers of vanquished enemies. The NKPA and the CCP would almost always attack any sector other than those guarded by the Turks. On the western side of the peninsula, the Turkish Brigade was able to delay the CCP Army a full two days at the end of November, and that allowed most UN forces to withdraw safely.

The Eighth Army fought numerous delaying actions and strategic withdrawals southward back past P'yongyang and even farther. Following a scorched earth policy, they left nothing behind that the CCP and NKPA could use. Bridges, electrical lines, roads, farms—everything was destroyed or taken. Even the weather was atrocious. Like the hot summer, the winter of 1950–51 was the coldest and one of the snowiest on record in Korea. In a freak jeep accident reminiscent of General Patton during WWII, General Walton Walker was killed on 23 December. General Matthew Ridgway was named commander of the Eight Army to replace him and soon had the troops stabilizing the lines. Then at the end of December, the CCP launched their Chinese New Year's offensive using night attacks accompanied by loud trumpets and gongs. At first, the UN forces bugged out in sheer panic. The NKPA and CCP armies pressed the attack and reoccupied Seoul on 4 January 1951. At that point, MacArthur considered using tactical nuclear weapons, but General Ridgway revitalized the troops and led a counteroffensive that brought them back to the Han River.

A series of seesaw attacks and operations occurred between both forces. Each UN counterstrike was provided a code name—Killer, Ripper, Courageous. With each successive attack and counterattack, the UN forces steadily marched north until 7 March when the Eighth Army retook Seoul. By this time, the air force was decimating the CCP and NKPA logistics support. An agreement between China and Russia resulted in Russia committing two air force brigades and hundreds of additional trucks to combat these air losses. But they were unsuccessful, and without reliable supplies making it to the front, the Red forces could not press a sustained attack.[44] The

---

44   In a telegram from Stalin to Kim Il-Sung dated 3 February 1951, he stated that Russia cannot supply lead to China and NK and asked Kim to restart lead

two battling armies settled into relatively stable defensive lines on the ground near the same locations as when the war began. As the ground war stagnated, the air war intensified with both Russian and Chinese MiGs now engaging the UN air service. In order to break the stalemate, General MacArthur wanted to expand the war by bombing strategic locations in China and using Taiwanese soldiers to fight the CCP. President Truman disagreed, and on 11 April 1951, he fired General MacArthur.

---

mines in the north and ship the ore to Russia. This shortage of lead for bullets may have contributed to the war stagnating.

SUMMER 2014

We received a response from Greg Gardner, the army's chief of Past Conflict Repatriations Branch (and Shorty Cox's boss), on 3 June 2014 that they had received our request to disinter X-739. Prior to our appeal and those of others submitted about the same time, there was no policy on how to process family requests to disinter unknown remains. Mr. Gardner included a new flow chart, dated 1 June 2014, that explained the complex review process that any request for disinterment would now follow. Basically, the Defense Prisoner of War/Missing Personnel Office (DPMO) would coordinate all such requests with the appropriate government agencies, including the Joint POW/MIA Accounting Command (JPAC), to review and decide whether to recommend or deny such requests. The final decision to disinter then would be decided by the appropriate command structure and based partly on the perceived probability that the remains exhumed could be identified. In X-739's case, that meant that the secretary of the army would make the final decision on whether or not to disinter centered on those recommendations.

The 2014 Korean / Cold War Annual Government Briefing on accounting initiatives was held on 14–15 August at the Hyatt Regency Crystal City near Reagan National Airport. Feeling ambitious after having attended a number of these briefings previously, we flew into Reagan and took the metro (subway) to Crystal City without renting a car. We felt that we could stay there and not have to fight traffic and walk, take a taxi, or ride the metro to get places if we needed. It worked out just fine.

This seminar, it was obvious that the DPMO was under pressure. Handouts for each of the presentations were provided in advance, all printed in color. Most were self-promotional, appearing to say how great DPMO was performing. Included in this seminar's general packet was information on new data from the Russians. Even though relations were strained at the time, the Joint Commission Support Division (JCSD) did have success gaining access to the Russian Central Archive of the Ministry of Defence (TsAMO), the Gulag files of the Russian Federation, and the military archives for WWII repatriation. They also gained limited access to the Ministry of Foreign Affairs, Ministry of Foreign Trade, and the Archive of Military Medical Records and museum. One tale they told was of trudging through six inches of water to retrieve documents from the flooded basement of the Central Archive of the Ministry of Defence in Podolsk, Russia. Over five hundred thousand pages of documents, plane gun camera films, photos of US plane crash sites and intelligence reports of the USSR Sixty-Fourth Corps were reviewed at Podolsk. Subject to intergovernmental relationship improvements, they hoped to gain access to the archives for the Russian president, the KGB/FSB, Ministry of Interior, and the Border Service of the Federal Security Service in the future. They also included four slides to show how their efforts did not support John Zimmerlee's suppositions in his book that American POWs were transferred to Russia during the Korean War.

A second related presentation told how the Soviets and, particularly Premier Joseph Stalin, controlled the Korean War, including the Chinese, through its generals and military advisors in order to gain information on US military technologies and capabilities. Though the Chinese had the manpower to intervene, they did not have the equipment until it was provided by the Soviets. They confirmed that the Soviets flew 74 percent of all communist sorties during the war—over seventy thousand Soviet servicemen actively serving combat duty in Korea. The Soviets deployed four antiaircraft artillery divisions and embedded numerous advisers in both NKPA and CCP infantry divisions and companies. The presenter related fascinating information garnered from their research through the archives about the Soviet view of the war. The Soviet stated that the Reds shot down as many UN planes as communist planes having been shot down—close to a 1:1 ratio. US statistics for the end of the war tell a different tale and indicate that the US shot down fourteen communist aircraft for every American plane shot down—a 14:1 ratio. The researchers also discovered multiple locations for airplane crash sights through this research that will receive visits for potential remains recovery when relations allow.

A follow-on presentation on DNA stated that as of the end of July 2014, fully 89 percent of the families of Korean War MIA/ POWs had provided DNA samples. New techniques were discussed on better demineralization of samples to improve results. Unluckily, the formaldehyde used to preserve unknown remains at Kokura encapsulates the DNA. AFMES (Armed Forces Medical Examiner System) has only been able to crack this encapsulation to gain sequenced DNA randomly one time out of many attempts. A separate presentation went through the efforts taken so far to sort out the mixed remains provided from North Korea using forensics and mtDNA analysis. In one case, 35 MIAs shared the same mtDNA and results could only be reduced to three based on forensics. Their conclusion was identification of these mixed returned remains would take a long time to complete. They did report that as of 4 August 2014, the unaccounted soldiers still missing from the Korean War had been reduced to 7,881 and 49 of the original buried Punchbowl unknowns had been identified.

We were scheduled to meet with our latest assigned army casualty officer late the afternoon of the first day. We were surprised when we arrived for the meeting that it was in a large room with six or seven other families and government representatives from related agencies. All the families in that room had requested disinterment of specific X-files remains from the Punchbowl backed by the research done by John Zimmerlee. The government wanted to reassure us that each case would be considered based on its merits, but it would take time. We also asked our casualty officer to confirm whether or not they had Donald Matney's dental chart, chest x-ray, and laundry mark and who else still missing might be associated with X-739. We never did receive any direct response from our casualty officer to these specific requests, though we did finally receive the answers.

That year's field trip was the most exciting of all. Six large airconditioned buses pulled up at the Hyatt at 5:00 p.m. along with half a dozen police cars and motorcycle cops. We left the hotel in a convoy escorted by the police. When we entered the Washington DC freeway system during rush hour, a seemingly never-ending supply of police cars and motorcycle cops redirected traffic so our convoy could make it from Crystal City to the Marine Barracks at Eighth and I Streets in downtown DC without stopping.

The Marine Barracks at Eighth and I is also known as the Oldest Post of the Corps, founded under President Thomas Jefferson in 1801. Among other marine traditions, it is the home of the famous Marine Band, the Marine Drum and Bugle Corps, and the Silent Drill Platoon. All three groups are entirely composed of marines on active duty, and most are noncommissioned officers. This is the post where John Philip Sousa wrote his famous patriotic marches, many of which are played every Friday night during the summer by the Marine Band. Free to the public with tickets, it is a spectacle of precision marching, flag waving, band playing, and arms drills. It is fun for all ages.

We also stayed an extra day that year to meet with a friend who was an army lieutenant colonel assigned to the Pentagon. After signing in and whisking through security, he took us on a personal tour of the Pentagon, including the internal chapel for the 9/11 memorial, his office outside the chief of the army, and the brass cafeteria. In the upper levels of the Pentagon, we saw many three- and four-star generals from all the service branches. We then visited the DC National Mall at night with him. Though it is something to see the Washington monuments during the day with the crowds and tourists, it is nothing compared to visiting at night when each monument can be seen, felt, and experienced practically alone. Most awe-inspiring was spending time at the Korean Memorial among the large statues of a platoon frozen in time on patrol. Also, of special note was the amount of detail and history encapsulated in the FDR (Franklin Delano Roosevelt) Memorial that can only be experienced when the crowds are sparse. Thanks, CP!

APRIL THROUGH
JULY 1951, KOREA

President Truman promoted General Matthew B. Ridgway to take General MacArthur's place as the supreme commander of the Allied powers in charge of all UN forces in Korea. Lieutenant General James Van Fleet was named commander of the Eighth Army. On April 15, with the ground war stagnant in fixed lines around the 38th parallel where the war began, the army started rotating soldiers who had served nine months in Korea back home. The rotations immediately increased morale on the front lines—the fighting soldier now knew that he had hope of returning home instead of fighting forever. Rotation home also brought experienced soldiers back to the training grounds to impart their experiences to the soldiers heading over to replace them. First Lieutenant Szito was rotated home on 8 July to become one of those trainers. He reverted in rank to master sergeant, but he was home. Finally, President Truman felt that there were enough troops and equipment in Korea to stop the CCP and NKPA without further expanding the war. As was becoming the case against communism elsewhere in the world, the war was now one of containment, not one of capturing the entire Korean peninsula or defeating the Chinese and Russians. But meanwhile the air war still raged.

UN forces used different fighter airplanes during the Korean War. It began with the deployment of the F-82 Twin Mustang, the last piston fighter plane acquired by the US. They were joined by straight-winged F-80 Shooting Star, F-84 Thunderjet, and Navy F9F

Panther jets. These planes worked against the North Korean People's Army Air Force (KPAAF) propeller-driven Yak-9s and Ilyushin Il-10 Shturmoviks in the early days of the war but were no match for the wing-swept Mikoyan-Gurevich MiG-15s moved to bases just north of the Yalu by the Russians. In order to combat these, the air force deployed the F-86 Sabre jet. Powered by a 5,910-pound thrust General Electric jet engine, the Sabre had a top speed of 693 mph and was typically armed with six .50-caliber machine guns.

The Russians deployed at least 450 MiG-15s at Chinese People's Liberation Army Air Force (PLAAF) bases just north of the Yalu River in the Antung/Sinuiju region of Manchuria. Flown at first only by the Russians, they could not fly south of the 38th parallel in fear of being shot down and the pilots' nationalities discovered. Likewise, the UN forces were limited to flying sorties south of the Yalu to stay out of China. So the first air-to-air battles between jets occurred in the northwest corner of North Korea in an area that quickly became known as MiG Alley.

The MiG-15 engine developed 5,000-pound thrust as designed and originally purchased from Rolls-Royce. That gave it a top speed of 668 mph. It had two 23 mm and one 37 mm cannons as armament. Compared to the F-86, it was slightly more maneuverable and had a higher service ceiling, but it was far less stable at high speeds and had a tendency to snap out of control in right-handed turns. Its gunsights were also decidedly inferior. Battles between the MiG-15 and F-86 Sabre depended mainly on the skills of the pilots involved. The duels between jet aircraft and piston propellers usually resulted in the loss of the slower piston plane. Officially, 2,714 American planes were shot down during the war and 4,055 airmen were killed. Many of these fatalities happened in the North and were never recovered.

But the CCP and NKPA were not finished on the ground. On 22 April 1951, just before nightfall, a shrieking, bugle-blowing human wave hurled at the lines of the Twenty-Fourth Infantry Division. Before they could unsling their bandoliers of grenades, these shock troops were slaughtered by machine guns, mines, and mortars. The second wave, consisting of burp-gun wielding, near-zombies, was also mowed down. Riflemen trailed and were also cut to ribbons. Bands of unarmed scavengers who grabbed a weapon from the fallen brought up the rear. For twenty-four hours, the Twenty-Fourth held its lines, killing thousands of CCP and NKPA soldiers. Finally, the Twenty-Fourth retired in a strategic withdrawal to prepared positions farther south. During that first twenty-four-hour period, Division artillery fired 15,712 rounds, the largest expenditure of cannon shells ever. The UN command stopped this first spring offensive and retreated only a few miles. The Twenty-Fourth Division claimed 32,875 enemy casualties.

The communists launched a second offensive by thirty divisions along a 105-mile battle line on 16 May. For three tragic days, CCP and NKPA forces flung thousands against mined approaches, barbed-wire aprons, and fortified bunkers. Sustaining enormous casualties, the attack developed into the most vicious pitched battle of the war. Entire enemy divisions were wiped out. With their supplies exhausted, the communist advance faltered, and the UN forces quickly counterattacked, forcing their way back to the same lines fought over at the beginning of January. The UN estimated that the CCP and NKPA lost over one hundred thousand casualties, twelve thousand prisoners, and expended vast quantities of ammunition and equipment to end up being pushed back to earlier positions. The communists suffered their worst defeat, bordering on catastrophic, since the beginning of the war.

One of the most fearsome weapons developed in WWII and heavily exploited in the Korean War and this battle was napalm. Used first by the air force by being dropped on charging enemy formations, it was devastating. The US infantry started using foo gas, as they called it, as a defensive weapon. Taking fifty-five-gallon drums of gasoline and adding twelve-gallons of thickener, they would dig holes and bury them in the approaches where they expected the enemy to attack. Set off remotely by an electrical charge, the resulting explosion could kill hundreds simultaneously by both the hot, searing contact of the flaming jelly and suffocate them by robbing the surrounding atmosphere of oxygen.

By the end of June, the ground war became a standstill with both sides digging in and making significant fortified defensive lines in depth. On 14 June, Mao conveyed his thoughts about an armistice in a letter[45] to Kim and Stalin. The Soviet ambassador to the UN broached the armistice idea during a radio speech in New York City on 23 June. In response, on 28 June, General Ridgway proposed meeting on a neutral Danish hospital ship in Wonsan harbor. The NKPA agreed to discussions on an armistice on 1 July in Kaesŏng.

---

45   https://digitalarchive.wilsoncenter.org/document/110365

SUMMER 2015

On 31 March 2015, the Department of Defense reorganized and disbanded the Defense Prisoner of War/ Missing Personnel Office (DPMO) and replaced it with the Defense POW/MIA Accounting Office (DPAA). The Joint POW/ MIA Accounting Command (JPAC) and Life Sciences Equipment Laboratory (LSEL) were integrated into it. A competent scientist replaced the politically appointed scientific director. The intent was to lessen infighting among departments and identify remains faster. The mission statement was set as this: "Provide the fullest possible accounting for our missing personnel to their families and the nation."[46] DPAA values were established to revolve around compassion, integrity, teamwork, respect, and innovation. The DPAA implemented its vision statement as this: "A world-class workforce fulfills our nation's obligation by maximizing the number of missing personnel accounted for while ensuring timely, accurate information is provided to their families."[47]

Shorty Cox also changed positions and became a mortuary affairs specialist, coordinating the communications with families when remains were identified. We received another letter from Greg Gardner dated 5 December 2014 that stated they were still reviewing our disinterment request and that Ms. Sherry Renz was now our contact for questions to replace Shorty Cox. This letter became the

---

46   www.dpaa.mil "Vision, Mission and Values" page

47   www.dpaa.mil "Vision, Mission and Values" page

official date for our request for disinterment even though we sent the original request to disinter on 25 April 2014. A duplicate letter was also sent dated 3 March 2015.

In 2015, instead of traveling back to Washington, DC, for the national update, we attended the regional update that was held in Denver, Colorado, on 16 May. The standard reports were provided, though in an abbreviated form. No special speakers attended to provide background, and there was no field trip. The program summarized that an additional thirty-five remains had been identified since the previous August, reducing the total unaccounted from Korea to 7,846.

We did meet with the army's casualty officer. Surprisingly, he provided us with additional new documents that reaffirmed our decision to request that the remains of X-739 be disinterred. These new unearthed documents included references to requests for dental records and comments that without them, Donald Matney could not be identified. Other documents referenced the possible association of X-739 with Donald Matney. Another new document, dated 16 January 1956, summarized the efforts taken to recover Donald Matney's remains and concluded that they were nonrecoverable as additional dental records had not been located. They also provided many of the same documents that we already received. Though in reality, we did not learn anything new, we felt reassured our request to disinter X-739 was the right one even if it turned out they were identified as another soldier.

JULY THROUGH DECEMBER 1951, KOREA

The first armistice meeting between the warring parties occurred at Kaesŏng on 8 July with the opening ceremonies held on 10 July. North Korea wanted that ancient city now within their lines as the location for the meeting for propaganda reasons as it made it appear that the UN was coming to them as petitioners asking for terms. The communists stayed in the stately buildings and mansions of the mostly undamaged historical city while the UN delegates stayed in tents nearby. During these first early days, it quickly became obvious that the communists were stalling and did not really want to negotiate. When the press train was stopped at the border, the UN recessed discussions in retaliation on 12 July to force the communist hand. From thence forth, the haughty and enigmatic communists stalled, hedged, and obstructed all discussions in order to gain any possible advantage, real or imagined, for propaganda purposes. Talks resumed on 15 July after the communists acceded that each delegation has equal press coverage and unhindered freedom of movement to and from the discussion location. Finally, on 26 July, both sides agreed upon a five-point discussion program:[48]

1. Adoption of an agenda
2. Establishing a military demarcation line
3. Arranging and supervising a ceasefire and armistice

---

48   Stadtmauer, *24th Forward*, 249.

4. Prisoner of War exchange
5. Other recommendations by concerned governments

But talks were not to last long as additional charges and countercharges stalled progress. Talks fell apart on 22 August. Finally, General Ridgway demanded that the conference be moved to a more neutral location, and on 25 October, the talks resumed in tents for both sides in a cow pasture near the small destroyed town of P'anmunjŏm, just a half a mile away from Kyu's small village of Taesŏng-tong.

The UN delegation objectives for the armistice discussions included the following:

- A demilitarized zone based on the tactical situation at the time of the armistice
- Security for the troops during ceasefire
- Guarantees against troop buildups during ceasefire
- Quick, satisfactory arrangements for all POWs

In his 14 November telegram to Stalin[49], Mao outlined the communist objectives as follows:

- A demilitarized zone at the original 38th parallel
- Ceasefire monitoring by noncombatant states of Poland, India, and USSR at one or two locations
- All for All POW exchange within three months
- Resolution of the Korean question by a joint conference after the armistice

Both sides postured mightily for their positions, and both sides thought the other was delaying progress. But finally, on 27 November 1951, a provisional demarcation line was agreed upon to be in effect for thirty days. The line zigzagged across the peninsula with historic Kaesŏng staying just inside the North Korean side. A demilitarized zone would be instituted on both sides of the line. However, talks broke down when discussions turned to ensuring a ceasefire and performing prisoner exchanges. The UN wanted to guarantee that the communists were not building up troops for another massive

---

49   https://digitalarchive.wilsoncenter.org/document/113013

attack during any ceasefire, and the communists wanted to be left to do whatever they wanted. As for prisoners, the UN desired to return one-for-one as many of the captured NKPA were impressed into service from the South and did not want to return to the North. The communists wanted an all-for-all exchange. While discussions continued, the UN requested that the Red Cross be allowed to inspect NK prison camps. North Korea denied this request. Finally, on 18 December, the communists produced a list of 11,559 names of prisoners, including 3,198 Americans. The UN provided a list of 132,474 Red prisoner names. As the communist newspapers had been boasting of 65,000 captured and with over 9,000 Americans missing, the communist list seemed to be lacking over 50,000 names. Newspapers around the world screamed that another mass extermination had occurred to the "unaccounted 50,000."[50] As the year wore on, the talks again stalled.

While the talks droned, the ground war stagnated. In early fall, all three regiments of the Twenty-Fourth Infantry were pulled off the front line and put into reserve training. Men were rotated on five-day leaves to the exotic resorts in Japan. While they were away, little happened on the lines, but the air war grew hotter. Bombers pounded factories, rail yards, and supply routes in the North. The NK side of the bridges across the Yalu to China were repeatedly bombed but stubbornly refused to fall. The North airfields were attacked again and again. If the NKPA objective for the talks was to stall for time to resupply the ground war anew, the air force was determined to stop them. To counter the UN air armada, the Russians started flying additional MiG sorties.

On 23 October, nine B-29 Superfortresses took off from Okinawa's Kadena airfield bound for the NK airfields at Namsi just south of the Yalu. Flying at twenty thousand feet that early morning, the B-29s formed three wedges of three and were joined by fifty-five close-cover Republic F-84 Thunderjets. As they got closer, thirty-two F-86 Sabre jets flew high cap at around thirty-five thousand feet. Flying on instruments, the B-29s lumbered toward their targets through major antiaircraft flak at Taechon. Two of the ships were hit. Once clear of the flak, the MiGs pounced. The Reds launched three groups of twenty MiGs each. Fourteen of the first group attacked

---

50   Stadtmauer, *24th Forward*, 260.

the thirty-two Sabre jets to keep them busy while the remaining six went after the lumbering B-29s. All twenty of the second group attacked the B-29s. The third group of 20 MiGs stayed in reserve across the Yalu in China and never engaged the Allied forces. The F-84 Thunderjets were no match for the MiGs and could not protect the B-29s. The thirty-two Sabre jets were completely occupied with the other 14 MiGs. In just under fifteen minutes, three B-29s were shot down, three were damaged so badly that they were scrapped after making emergency landings, and two more were heavily impaired but were able to return to service after many months of refurbishment. Only one returned safely to Okinawa with minor damage. More than 50 percent of the B-29 crewmen were killed or wounded during that foray. That was the last major daytime raid using propeller-driven bombers. The losses also forced the USAF to speed up a replacement for the propeller-driven planes[51] as they clearly could not continue to act as an effective nuclear deterrent.

Nighttime strategic bombing became the rule after that. Sure, the ground attack planes still performed during the day attacking troop movements, trains, and trucks. But the big strategic bombing runs against bridges, factories, and airfields were now performed during darkness as the MiGs had no internal radar to locate and shoot down the bombers. Bomber losses were reduced but accuracy suffered, and targets often required multiple sorties. The air force was successful in keeping the skies controlled by the UN except for the contested MiG Alley. Bombing raids South by the communists were unsuccessful and limited to Bedcheck Charlie planes dropping minor, inaccurate bombs. Though the communists spent almost seven months digging in and fortifying their defensive lines, neither side launched any major offensives. The battle lines stayed the same as when established in July.

The Twenty-Fourth Infantry Taro Leaf returned to forward positions in early October 1951. They mounted a minor offensive to grab a communist ammunition depot near Kumsong. Then they settled in and built defenses in depth. Intimidation by searchlight and strategic barrage by massed cannons and missiles while improving defensive positions was the typical day during this lull in the ground war.

---

51   The B-47 Stratojet swept wing six-jet high-altitude medium bomber entered service in 1952 to replace the B-36.

SPRING 2016

PAA started analyzing whether to exhume X-739 in the middle of 2015. That summer, 186 unidentified and unresolved casualties were outstanding from the Battle of Taejon. Of these, only 55 had no known POW associations. The 131 associated with being captured were excluded from analysis as it would be improbable that any would have been buried south of Taejon along the escape route where X-739 had been found. Sixteen cases of the remaining 55 fit the general dental parameters of X-739. Of these, only 12 fit the race, age, and stature identified for X-739. These included 4 from the Nineteenth Infantry with two from H Company—Corporal Joe Madril and Corporal Donald Matney. Last seen reports for these twelve individuals placed seven of them in Taejon proper, three south of town (including Donald Matney), and two along the escape route to Okch'on where X-739 was located. For some reason, Donald Matney was listed as last seen taking the southern escape route that the Nineteenth Infantry Second Regiment used instead of going through town with the rest of Howe Company. How this was determined was never divulged. One of these twelve remaining MIAs was eliminated during analysis due to a comparison of surviving dental x-rays to X-739 file pictures. Based on this historical analysis, DPAA concluded that there was a better than 50 percent probability that the remains of X-739 could be positively identified if they were examined as one of the 11 remaining missing soldiers. In a memorandum for record dated 16 September 2015, DPAA recommended to the secretary of the army that X-739 be exhumed.

In early March 2016, we received an e-mail from Shorty Cox confirming that the secretary of the army had approved the disinterment of X-739 for the purpose of performing an updated autopsy and modern identification procedure. The e-mail further explained that every protocol would be followed to ensure that the remains were treated with dignity and respect throughout the disinterment and identification process. He further explained that the process may take many months and that there were no guarantees that the remains would be identified as Corporal Donald Matney or any other individual but that he would contact us at a later date with news and progress on the process.

Once a disinterment has been approved, the remains are exhumed by DPAA with a full honor guard present. The DPAA honor guards consist of six soldiers plus an officer. Guards are from any branch of the service and include both men and women. Once the casket is raised, a US flag is draped over it, and the six guards slowly carry it to a hearse for transport to the DPAA laboratory. An honor guard stays with the remains throughout the journey. X-739 was disinterred on 16 May 2016 following this process and accessioned as CIL 2016-068-I-01 for identification purpose at the DPAA Laboratory.

The DPAA Laboratory in Hawaii is the largest and most diverse skeletal identification lab in the world. More than thirty anthropologists, archaeologists, and forensic odontologists staff it. Upon arrival in the lab, all remains and material evidence are signed over to an evidence coordinator and stored in secure, locked areas. Usually, the scientists assigned to the analysis do not know the suspected identity of the remains. Specific details are provided concerning the time and locale where the remains were founded to allow the scientists to select the appropriate scientific techniques without influencing their results. First, a biological profile is made of the skeleton to determine the sex, race, stature, and age at death. Possible trauma caused at or near the time of death is identified as well as earlier healed broken bones. Along with physical evidence, a profile is then created to compare against possible missing-in-action candidates. If possible, a DNA sample is taken and submitted to the Armed Forces DNA Identification Laboratory for analysis and comparison. If the skull and teeth are present, a full dental chart is made. X-rays may also be taken of the teeth and torso for comparison to any existing dental and chest radiographs. All reports go through an extensive peer review, including an external review by independent experts and review by the second DPAA lab in Omaha, Nebraska.

Forensic Anthropology Report: CIL 2016-068-I-01

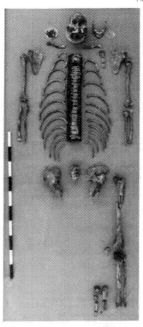
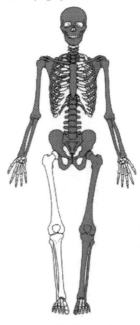

Figure 1. CIL 2016-068-I-01, skeletal layout. Scale is in decimeters.

Figure 2. CIL 2016-068-I-01, skeletal diagram. Elements in red are present. Present teeth, unseriated proximal pedal phalanx, and perimortem damage not depicted.

X-739 Skeletal Remains

In the review of X-739, DPAA provided the scientists performing the analysis with the charts and historical information for the eleven potential candidates identified during the case for exhumation. This would allow them to compare the remains quickly and eliminate or affirm each of the candidates without duly influencing their opinion toward any specific candidate.

Dr. Ivett Kovari, PhD, conducted the forensic anthropology report. He first noted the condition of the remains and the efforts taken to reconstruct them. The skeleton was reported as being mostly complete with the left leg, both hands, and most of the bones from the feet missing. He recorded that the left tibia was sampled for DNA analysis, which was unsuccessful due to the remains having been treated with formaldehyde. The reports stated that the remains were consistent with being from one individual. Various other measurements and tests indicated that the skeleton was male with a high degree of certainty. Age-related benchmarks of epiphyseal fusion set the estimated age between 16 and 20 with a mean age of 19.4 based on data for Korean War–era American soldiers. Analysis of the skull midface indicated that the skeleton was of European ancestry. Measurements of the left tibia and fibula put the stature at 66.7" +/- 2.7". Projectile trauma was evident on the cranium, possible blunt force or projectile trauma was noted to the ribs, and other blunt force trauma may have occurred in six other locations. The report addendum compared the measurements with Corporal Donald Matney and concluded that there were no major differences.

The dental analysis was performed by the odontologist Dr. Colin A. Eliot, DMD, LCDR, DC, USN. Dr. Eliot took numerous photographs and physically examined the maxilla and mandible of X-739. He noted that tooth no. 4 on the remains was impacted and was covered by teeth no. 3 and no. 5 in life. All three teeth were manually charted as present along with the wisdom teeth in Corporal Matney's original exam, performed when he first entered the army on 17 August 1949 for basic training. However, X-739 had no wisdom teeth and no. 4 was impacted. Dr. Eliot surmised that the wisdom teeth were extracted after the early manual exam and the impacted no. 4 was just mischarted as no. 3 and no. 5 covered it cleanly. Dr. Eliot summarized that the dental remains of CIL 2016-068-I-01 were possibly those of Corporal Donald Matney.

A blind chest radiograph comparison was completed by Emily Wilson, MA, an anthropologist, against the ten available chest x-rays from the eleven identified potential candidates for X-739. Prior to the Korean War, all inductees were given a chest x-ray to check for tuberculosis, and the original photos for ten of the eleven candidates survived the 1973 fire at the National Personnel Records Center (NPRC) in St. Louis. Posteroanterior chest radiograph identification was a new process where skeletal remains were reconstructed using modeling clay and then x-rayed in the same position as was performed back in the late 1940s. These X-rays can then be sized similar to original x-rays in surviving army medical records and compared. Clavicles (collar bones) are similar to fingerprints as no two appear to be alike. Measurements on sizes, angles, breaks, and connections can be compared to older x-rays and properly sized negatives can be overlaid. Ms. Wilson compared all ten surviving candidates' chest x-rays and the reconstructed CIL 2016-068-I-01 x-ray. None matched except Donald E. Matney's. Not only did the clavicles match but the articulations of vertebrae C4 through T3 were the same. Ms. Wilson concluded that the exhumed CIL 2016-068-I-01 remains, also known as X-739, were indeed Donald E. Matney.

Chest Radiograph Comparison Report: CIL 2016-068-I-01

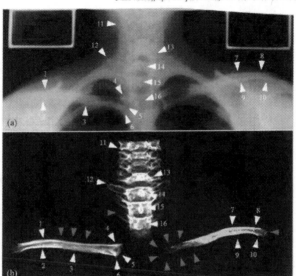

Figure 3. CIL 2016-068-I-01, juxtaposed comparison to Cpl MATNEY's AM radiograph: (a) Cpl MATNEY's exposure-enhanced AM radiograph; and (b) PM radiograph from CIL 2016-068-I-01. For a description of the 16 items of concordance, see Table 2. Gray arrows on (b) indicate areas with postmortem damage.

X-739 Chest X-Ray comparison

JANUARY 1952 THROUGH JULY 1953, KOREA

On 16 January 1952, word came down that the entire Twenty-Fourth Infantry "Taro Leaf" Division was withdrawing from battle in Korea and returning to garrison duty in Japan. The Fortieth "Sunburst" Division would take its place on the lines facing the NKPA and CCP. On the appointed date, the Nineteenth Regiment shouldered its gear, left the heavy guns and mortars in place, and headed south for transport to Japan. After eighteen long months and many battles, Captain Reagan withdrew safely from the war, scarred only by his memory. The Twenty-Fourth Division retired to five camps on the main island of Honshu and resumed guard duties instead of combat.

The war persisted another nineteen long months as the two sides sparred while negotiating at P'anmunjŏm. The UN still controlled the skies (except for MiG Alley) and bombed and strafed Red logistics and troops at will. Major battles were fought, including the Battle of Old Baldy (26 June–4 August 1952), the Battle of White Horse (6–15 October 1952), the Battle of Triangle Hill (14 October–25 November 1952), the Nevada Outposts Counterattack (26–30 March 1953), the Battle of Outpost Harry (10–18 June 1953), the Battle of Pork Chop Hill (23 March–16 July 1953), and the Battle of Kumsong (13–27 July 1953) that was fought right up until the armistice was signed. There were many casualties on both sides as the communists thought that a war of attrition would sap the will of the Americans to fight. In reality, these battles accomplished nothing except the death of the boys who gave their lives. The lines seesawed back and forth but only varied by a few miles from when the war first began.

Both sides also performed psychological warfare, or psyops, to try to convince members from the other side to defect or at least quit fighting. Leaflets were created and dropped from airplanes or fired from cannons. During one day in November 1950, US bombers dropped 1.2 million "safe conduct passes" and 1.4 million "good treatment of prisoners" leaflets printed in both Chinese and Korean. Two days later, the Reds retaliated by dropping thousands of leaflets saying that they treated POWs well, and it was needless to die so far from home. Trailer-mounted speakers were another favorite of both sides, blasting soothing music intermixed with rhetoric. Mobile radios were also used with the NKPA broadcasting for an hour daily and the Chinese for 3.5 hours daily on nineteen different frequencies. While the NKPA controlled Seoul at the beginning of the war, Seoul City Sue broadcasted music and propaganda almost continuously. UN forces also broadcasted propaganda aimed at both the NKPA and Chinese from South Korea, Japan, and from ships sailing along the shoreline.

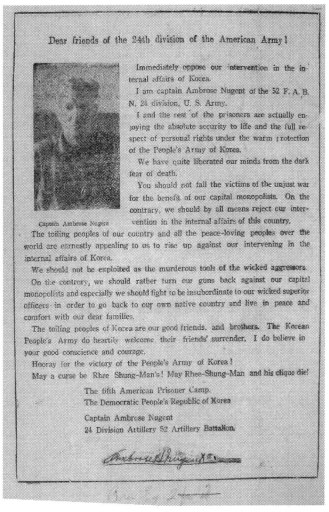

Dear friends of the 24th division of the American Army!

Immediately oppose our intervention in the internal affairs of Korea.

I am captain Ambrose Nugent of the 52 F. A. B. N. 24 division, U. S. Army.

I and the rest of the prisoners are actually enjoying the absolute security to life and the full respect of personal rights under the warm protection of the People's Army of Korea.

We have quite liberated our minds from the dark fear of death.

You should not fall the victims of the unjust war for the benefit of our capital monopolists. On the contrary, we should by all means reject our intervention in the internal affairs of this country.

The toiling peoples of our country and all the peace-loving peoples over the world are earnestly appealing to us to rise up against our intervening in the internal affairs of Korea.

We should not be exploited as the murderous tools of the wicked aggressors.

On the contrary, we should rather turn our guns back against our capital monopolists and especially we should fight to be insubordinate to our wicked superior officers in order to go back to our own native country and live in peace and comfort with our dear families.

The toiling peoples of Korea are our good friends, and brothers. The Korean People's Army do heartily welcome their friends' surrender. I do believe in your good conscience and courage.

Hooray for the victory of the People's Army of Korea!

May a curse be Rhee Shung-Man's! May Rhee-Shung-Man and his clique die!

The fifth American Prisoner Camp.
The Democratic People's Republic of Korea

Captain Ambrose Nugent
24 Division Artillery 52 Artillery Battalion.

Captain Ambrose Nugent

NKPA Propaganda dropped 20-Jul-1950

Meanwhile, negotiations plodded on at P'anmunjŏm. The communists battled the UN on every little detail, from lines on a map to room decorations, and levied complaints about any perceived wartime violation strictly for propaganda purposes. They also practiced intimidation tactics to gain perceived psychological advantages. They often had their guards snarl menacingly with their weapons fully cocked and primed. They cut the legs shorter on the UN delegates' chairs to make them sit lower at the table. They replaced the NK flags with larger ones to make the North seem more important in pictures.

The North Korean stone-faced lead negotiator once famously sat impassively for five minutes while a fly crawled across his face. They tried any little thing to gain minor advantage for propaganda purposes.

From the outset, the communists wanted a ceasefire before discussing an armistice. This was purely to allow them to rearm and to buy time. This was proven during the thirty-day review of the original proposed demarcation line when the NKPA feverously built defenses and resupplied their army. Another sticking point was the repatriation of POWs. The communists wanted all POWs returned as the impressed soldiers from the South would be used as slaves and viewed as wanting to return to the virtues of communism. The UN wanted to allow each prisoner the option to stay or return. By the spring of 1952, UN forces questioned whether the Reds were even serious about ceasing hostilities. Finally, in October 1952, the UN unilaterally ended negotiations.

Back in the States, Dwight D. Eisenhower was elected president in November 1952. Being the five-star general who won the war in Europe, he publicly discussed escalating the war and allowing Taiwan to bomb targets in mainline China. He even discussed using nuclear weapons and let slip information about the test results from a miniaturized nuclear cannon shell. He approved the ROK Army expansion from fourteen divisions to twenty divisions. Eisenhower also removed the Seventh Fleet from patrolling the China Sea, thus removing the US as a buffer between China and Taiwan. He was subtly telling China that a second battlefront may be needed to end the conflict. Then suddenly on 5 March 1953, Joseph Stalin died and Georgy Malenkov assumed power in the USSR. Mao Zedong, the Chinese leader, no longer had the senior Stalin to support and dictate his actions through the control of critical war supplies. Zhou Enlai attended Stalin's funeral and asked the USSR to help conclude the Korean talks. The USSR Council of Ministers under Malenkov on 19 March proposed new negotiation positions to Mao and Kim.[52]

To the surprise of the UN, on 28 March, the NKPA asked to resume negotiations. They promptly agreed to a neutral commission to decide the fate of the POWs. The communists wanted to preserve the propaganda victories, especially the perception that they had beaten back the great Western powers for the first time in over a

---

52   https://digitalarchive.wilsoncenter.org/document/113649

hundred years. Moving relatively fast now, on 11 April 1953, they agreed to exchange sick and wounded POWs. Lasting from 20 April through 3 May, Operation Little Switch saw the exchange of 6,670 communist prisoners and 684 UN prisoners, including the return of 149 Americans. By 27 April, negotiations resumed in earnest, and the UN was shocked that the Reds seemed ready to end hostilities. This scared President Rhee[53] of South Korea who, like MacArthur, believed that only total victory would suffice and that Korea should be reunited as a single country. Eisenhower appeased Rhee by guaranteeing a mutual security pact, long-term economic aid, and the resources to complete the expansion of ROK forces to twenty divisions.

In the longest peace negotiations ever completed, after 158 meetings spread over two years and seventeen days, an armistice agreement was reached on 27 July 1953. Not saying a word, a ranking general from each side met at the table in P'anmunjŏm and signed the agreement. Hostilities ended that night at 2200. It is important to note that the agreement was not endorsed by any government and signed only by generals from the two factions. Technically, North and South Korea are still at war.

The agreement suspended all open hostilities. It withdrew all military forces and equipment from a four-thousand-meter-wide demilitarized zone (DMZ) as a buffer spread across the peninsula. It prevented the forces from entering the air, ground, or sea of the opponent. It agreed to the release and repatriation of POWs and displaced personnel coordinated by neutral parties, and it created the Military Armistice Commission (MAC) and other agencies to discuss any violations to ensure adherence to the truce terms. Only two small towns would be inhabited within the DMZ: Kijŏng-dong on the north side and Kyu's Taesŏng-tong on the south.

---

53 Rhee's statement on 6 June 1953 requested a mutual defense pact—US forces stay in Korea and US supply Korea with military equipment.

FALL 2016

My wife, Sandy, started to cry after receiving that telephone call in early August 2016. Shorty Cox, now a DPAA mortuary affairs specialist, told her that X-739 had definitely been identified as her uncle, Corporal Donald Matney. He said that the specialists out in Hawaii concluded that the remains were his after an exhaustive examination and peer review. He stated a book containing the test reports and analysis would be available to review their conclusions. He wanted to set up a meeting with Sandy's aunt Ruth, the oldest surviving next of kin, and us sometime after October 1, the beginning of a new government fiscal year when travel money would become available. We agreed to meet in Seymour, Missouri, Uncle Donnie's old hometown, on 19 October.

19 July 2016

The remains designated CIL 2016-068-I-01, DPAA 2016-0073 are identified as those of

Corporal Donald Eugene MATNEY; RA 17273184; U.S. Army

Copy editing and quality assurance procedures may result in some reports post dating the identification date.

EDWARD A. REEDY, Ph.D., M.D. (D-ABP)
Captain, Medical Corps, U.S. Navy
Science Director
Defense POW/MIA Accounting Agency

Enclosures (10):

1. Memorandum for Record: Association of Unknown X-739 Tanggok With Eleven Unresolved Korean War Casualties; dtd 16 September 2015
2. Historical Report: Field Search Case 016-F Vicinity of Changnyong, North Kyongsang Province, Republic of Korea; dtd 11 July 2016
3. Forensic Odontology Report: CIL 2016-068-I-01; dtd 10 June 2016
4. Forensic Anthropology Report: CIL 2016-068-I-01; 5 July 2016
5. Forensic Anthropology Report Addendum: CIL 2016-068-I-01; dtd 1 August 2016
6. Chest Radiograph Comparison Report: CIL 2016-068-I-01; dtd 31 May 2016
7. Relevant Personnel Records
8. AGO Form 0353, Finding of Death of Missing Person; Corporal Donald E. Matney; undtd
9. DD2064, Certificate of Death Overseas, MATNEY, Donald Eugene; dtd 19 July 2016
10. Consultant's Comments: CIL 2016-068-I-01; MATNEY, Donald E.; dtd 28 August 2016

DPAA Letter Affirming X-739 as Donald Matney

By this time, ninety-nine-year-old Aunt Ruth was quite frail and had been living in a nursing home bedridden for several months. Her only remaining sibling, Donnie's younger brother Leonard, came to visit her at least daily. We flew from Denver to Kansas City, rented a car, and drove the three hours to Seymour. We stayed nearby in Marshfield at The Dickey House Bed and Breakfast. After a wonderful gourmet breakfast, we drove with Uncle Leonard to Aunt Ruth's nursing home. Surprisingly, she was up and dressed and as spry as an eighty-year-old. Shorty Cox came in with assigned casualty officer SFC Robert Belles from Fort Leonard Wood nearby.

Shorty Cox provided each of us with a colored booklet more than sixty pages in length that contained the complete reports, analysis, and background on the identification process the DPAA performed to identify X-739 as Donald Matney. We reviewed the highlights and saw the results, supporting evidence, and outside independent assessment that concluded that it actually was him. Aunt Ruth was ecstatic! She kept bringing up tales and memories she had of Uncle Donnie and would not let Shorty Cox leave. Though he could be buried anywhere, including Arlington National Cemetery, we decided to hold the reburial on 19 November in the plot that Aunt Anna had reserved for Donnie next to his mother's grave in the Seymour Masonic Cemetery. As Aunt Ruth couldn't do it, we also made Uncle Leonard the next of kin to coordinate the ceremony with the help of casualty officer SFC Robert Belles.

On 18 November, we drove to St. Louis, Missouri, to greet the return of Uncle Donnie's remains at the airport and to travel with them to Seymour. When we got to the private hangar where Uncle Donnie was to arrive, we were surprised to see two large fire engine ladder trucks parked across the parking lot entrance with their ladders fully extended into the air and a 9×15-foot flag hanging between them. A fire crew was also on hand for both trucks in full dress uniforms. About a dozen different police cars—including city, county sheriff, and state troopers—were also gathered. And twenty or so Patriot Guards were on hand with their motorcycles to accompany the processional. News crews and reporters were standing by to film the arrival, including filming from a helicopter. Missouri was treating Uncle Donnie's arrival home after sixty-six years as an important event. Governor Nixon ordered the flags in the state to half-mast for 19 November in his honor. Representative Vicky Hartzler recognized him in the *Congressional Record*, and as we would soon discover, the people of Missouri would go all out to welcome this missing serviceman home.

Cpl Donald Matney arrives in St. Louis

Donnie's remains were transferred from the DPAA Laboratory to the Honolulu airport in a hearse by an honor guard. A sergeant first class in dress uniform was his escort and traveled with him throughout his journey to the funeral home in Seymour. The escort ensured that the casket was handled properly and with respect throughout the journey. He saw to it that the casket was covered with a flag and flew headfirst inside each plane. He was the first off each flight and slow hand saluted as the casket was transferred. They flew together from Honolulu to Atlanta and then to St. Louis. Once in St. Louis, the escort privately examined the uniform and remains in the casket and rearranged them to ensure that they were perfect. An honor guard from Fort Leonard Wood met the escort and Uncle Donnie in the private hangar. They slowly marched him out of the hangar in his flag-draped casket to a waiting hearse. The police and Patriot Guard lined the way and saluted as he was carried. We followed behind as the family representatives.

Under scattered showers, the processional formed up with various police leading the way interspersed with Patriot Guards on motorcycles, the honor guard, hearse, us, and the various press. We drove under the fire truck–suspended flag as the firemen saluted and started on I-44 for the 211-mile drive to Seymour. With lights flashing, the processional progressed at a stately pace. Nearly every bridge and overpass held people waving flags and saluting as we drove underneath. Many bridges held fire engines and police with lights flashing on top.

We turned off at Rolla where the local fire department paid tribute by hanging a flag between two ladder trucks. Traveling on US 63 and all along the route, we noticed folks pulled off along the side of the road silently paying their respects. We stopped again in Kabool where we were met by a young couple who presented us with a shadow box in honor of Uncle Donnie's sacrifice. Additional cars added to the processional, including a number of 1950s classic automobiles. We then traveled on US 60 where again folks stopped on both sides of the freeway and lined the bridges and overpasses to pay their respects. The closer we came to Seymour, the more people lined the highway. The bridges at Mountain Grove and Norwood were lined with veterans, police, firemen, and ordinary citizens. Our daughter and family joined us in the processional just outside of Seymour where hundreds of cars and people lined the streets as we drove to the funeral home. How all these folks had learned about the processional and when and where it would be, I will never know. That they came to honor a serviceman none knew from sixty years ago is to be commended.

Uncle Leonard and SFC Robert Belles met us at the funeral home. Again, the escort privately examined Uncle Donnie. The casket was split into two levels with Uncle Donnie's remains in the lower half and a class A dress uniform adorned with his medals in the upper half. Dog tags were included with both the uniform and on the outside of the casket. SFC Robert Belles also provided Uncle Leonard with copies of Donald Matney's military awards and medals. Corporal Matney was awarded a Purple Heart, an Army Good Conduct medal, Army of Occupation Medal with a Japan Clasp, National Defense Service Medal, Korean Service Medal with one bronze service star, a Presidential Unit Citation medal, the Combat Infantryman Badge, a United Nations Service Medal, and a Korean War Service Medal and Republic of Korea Presidential Unit Citation. After staying awake for over twenty-seven hours, the escort from Honolulu was exhausted. SFC Robert Belles volunteered to drive him to Springfield, Missouri, to allow him to sleep overnight before catching a flight the next morning back to Hawaii. Corporal Donald Matney's flag-draped coffin was arrayed overnight in a side alcove at the Holman-Howe Funeral Homes. Another funeral of significance was being held in the main hall.

Cpl Donald Matney's horse drawn caisson

19 November proved to be a cool, crisp fall morning in Seymour and bright with sunshine. We drove with our daughter's family to the funeral home and met Uncle Leonard and SFC Robert Belles there by 1000. By this time, Aunt Ruth was too frail to travel and slept most of the time and could not attend the burial. The honor guard from Fort Leonard Wood hand carried the flag-draped casket from the alcove to a horse-drawn caisson. We then slowly trekked from the funeral home the ¾ mile to the cemetery behind the caisson and the marching armed honor guard. Again, the street was lined with silent people paying their respects, many with American flags in hand. Two hook and ladder fire engines with a large American flag hung between their extended ladders waited silently behind the graveyard. Hundreds attended the graveside service. Special seats were set up for the family and dignitaries. Rev. Mark Terrill of Seymour Nazarene Church read stirring words. Along with a folded flag, special awards were presented to Uncle Leonard on behalf of the army, the state of Missouri, the American Legion, and the Patriot Guards. Taps were played and shots were fired. Probably the best summary of the service can be found courtesy of television station KY3 in Springfield at https://www.ky3.com entitled *The Three Burials of Corporal Donald Matney*.[54] Afterward, those attending paid their respects to the family.

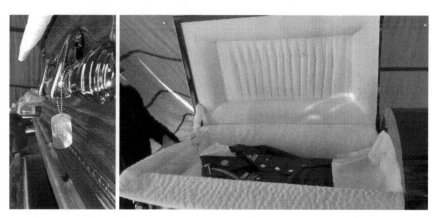

One of those paying respects was a middle-aged lady who told us her dad knew Donald Matney and had always wondered what had happened to him. In fact, her father had just passed away and was to

---

54   *The Three Burials of Corporal Donald Matney*, Drew Douglas, KY3 News, 19
      November 2016.

be buried that same afternoon in the same cemetery. His was the other funeral at Holman-Howe Funeral Home. She was glad he had learned of Uncle Donnie's fate before he died. His name was Joe Peters, and he told her that he had driven Uncle Donnie and Chuck Farr to the train station in August 1950 when they enlisted and were leaving for basic training. He was only sixteen at the time, and his mom would not allow him to join his friends as they left for the army. Donald Matney and Joseph Peters spent their last night together in the same funeral home and were buried the same day in the same cemetery sixty-six years after leaving each other as friends at the train station.

1954 KOREA

Woo Kyu-Chul, his wife, Nabi, their five-year-old daughter, Sa-rang, and their three-year-old son, victorious Seung, came home to Taesŏng-tong in the spring of 1954 after Kyu was discharged from the army. Their farmhouse, *oeyang-gan* (barn), and all the *non* (rice fields) nearby had been destroyed. Only those whose families had lived in Taesŏng-tong prior to the war were allowed to return. The government provided them with generous loans and incentives to rebuild, and the army sent guards to make sure that the North Koreans did them no harm, living as they were inside of the DMZ. Kyu and Nabi were able to rebuild and enjoyed a long and prosperous life together in the land between two nations. Their rice, like others in Taesŏng-tong, was sought after and garnered a premium when sold in the markets.

The Korean War, or the June 25th War as it is known in the ROK, was relatively short—lasting just three and a half years—but exceptionally bloody. Almost 5,000,000 people lost their lives during this quick war, including at least 1,500,000 civilians—over 5% of the total Korean population. The United States officially lists 36,923 killed or missing in action and 716,000 wounded. Over 217,000 ROK personnel lost their lives. After fighting for three years, South Korea gained an additional 1,500 square miles of land while North Korea acquired the ancient capital city of Kaesŏng. The dividing line between the two countries is still near the 38th parallel as originally arbitrarily set at the end of WWII. Of course, both sides declared the end of the war a victory.

Operation Big Switch to exchange additional prisoners began in August 1953 and ran through December. During that time, the Reds repatriated 12,773 POWs to the UN, and the UN returned 75,823 prisoners to the Reds. Those returned included 3,597 Americans. Over 22,600 Red POWs did not want to return, and surprisingly, 23 Americans and 1 Brit also did not want to be repatriated. The belligerents were allowed ninety days to try to convince those who did not want to return to change their minds following the exchange. There were 137 Chinese and 2 Americans who changed their minds. Officially, 8,154 Americans remained as missing in action at the close of the war after Operation Big Switch. Of these, at least 3,260, and maybe as high as 4,116, were thought to be lost behind enemy lines and possibly alive as POWs during the war. Soldiers returning from the war were cautioned not to talk about this so as not to stir up sentiment and cause the communists to take action in case any were still alive. This may be one reason the Korean War is often called the Forgotten War - the returning veterans did not talk about it.

The Soviets historically desired the Korean peninsula and wanted it to be part of their sphere of influence. Back in 1895, prior to their defeat in the Russian-Japanese War, Korea's king ruled from the Russian ligation in Seoul. Stalin thought he had his chance to rule Korea again at the end of WWII. Stalin did not declare war against Japan until 8 August 1945, two days after the first atomic bomb was dropped on Hiroshima. However, he committed over a million soldiers to Manchuria to defeat the Japanese before declaring war. These soldiers bashed their way through the Japanese, quickly advancing toward the Korean peninsula. Seeing how fast the Russians were advancing, two young officers, Dean Rusk and Charles Bonesteel, used a *National Geographic* map to arbitrarily choose the 38th parallel as the dividing line between Soviet and US influence. They did not know that the 38th parallel was the same line previously discussed between Russia and Japan prior to their war at the turn of the century. They were surprised when Stalin quickly agreed to that arbitrary line.

Based on comments made after the end of WWII by US diplomats, Stalin thought the US would never intervene and the North under Kim would invade the South and be quickly victorious. Had it not been for General MacArthur, they would have been correct. It was due solely to MacArthur's convincing arguments to the Joint Chiefs of Staff and President Truman that ground troops were engaged to stop the NKPA offensive. The distance-for-time strategy employed by the Twenty-Fourth Division was his and General Walker's idea, and it was due solely to him that the Inchon landing occurred that started a second front that kicked the NKPA out of the South. McArthur's command was ill prepared and out of shape when the NLPA attacked, but McArthur overcame these shortfalls in time. Though he was despised by many, MacArthur's perseverance changed the course of Korean history.

MacArthur always suspected that the Soviets were behind the invasion. As early as 27 June, two days after the invasion, the South Koreans were claiming that five out of ten tanks that they captured or knocked out were manned by mixed NKPA and Russian troops. During the opening salvo when US planes were evacuating dependents from Kimpo Airport, one of four enemy planes shot down had a red star on it indicating that the plane came from the Soviets. Pilots during those opening air battles also noted a plane flying low near Kimpo traveling in excess of four hundred miles per hour. Only a Soviet jet could attain those speeds. On 26 June, the South Korean Navy also sunk small corvette ships reported to be Soviet. High Korean officials, including the ambassador to the US, stated that the communist invasion could not have been staged without the direct assistance of Soviet Russia. MacArthur had this intelligence when he conferenced with Truman and the Chiefs of Staff via teletype on 29 June 1950.

MacArthur and Truman at Wake Island

The Korean War was also the first time US ground troops were integrated. Black soldiers fought side by side with whites, including intermixed in the Nineteenth Infantry Regiment. The communists also learned that the US would fight a limited war, leading to tactics that they would successfully exploit later in Vietnam. The Korean War also helped break the fifty-year hold the Democratic Party had on the US presidency, contributing to the election of Dwight D. Eisenhower.

But was the Korean War worth the lives of over thirty-six thousand Americans and the billions of dollars spent?

2017 KOREA

Every year since 2010, the Korean Ministry of Patriots and Veterans Affairs (MPVA) has flown Korean War veterans and their family representatives to the Republic of Korea. Their intent is to express the gratitude of the Korean people for their sacrifices and to show how Korea has enjoyed peace and prosperity because of it. We were lucky to be selected to attend the spring 2017 visit with over fifty Americans representing twenty-seven MIA or KIA veterans.

After flying into Seoul, we joined an orientation and Korean cultural experience that taught us basic Korean history and culture. We learned Korean phrases and tried on traditional *hanbok* wedding attire. As it was Memorial Day[55] the following Monday in the States, we traveled to the Korean National Cemetery where we helped place a wreath in memory of those lost during the war. There we also visited the Ministry of National Defense Agency for KIA Recovery and Identification (MAKRI), the Korean equivalent of DPAA. In a hot, crowded conference room, MAKRI provided an update on their efforts to locate additional remains from the war. At the ceremony of the fallen soldiers in the Korean War, Sandy received a tribute for Uncle Donnie's sacrifice. We traveled to the site of the Nevada Outposts Counterattack for a demonstration of Korean Army precision and drill teams, including a very impressive martial arts display. The young men participating went all-out as we noticed many had cuts, bruises, and bandages after the ceremony. We also attended a

---

55   Korean Memorial Day is always 6 June.

traditional Korean picnic lunch and met with members of the Korean military, who were all very open, honest, and polite. At The War Memorial of Korea, we were able to take pencil etchings of Donald Matney's placard along with pictures of the impressive monument.

We then rode buses to the Demilitarized Zone (DMZ) and visited the historical site of P'anmunjŏm where the armistice was finally signed. Once farmland and subsequently a devastated battleground, the DMZ is now one of the most pristine, undeveloped land masses in all of Asia. Some 3,500 different plants, mammals, birds, and fishes have been identified in the DMZ and Civilian Control Zone (CCZ) around it, including more than 80 protected species, like Asiatic black bears, lynxes, and endangered white-naped and red-crowned cranes. Of course, there are also unexploded antipersonnel mines and remains from the war, and three-legged deer are not uncommon. There, Colonel Steve Lee, in charge of the United Nations Command Security Battalion-Joint Security Area, briefed us on the current situation with North Korea. When we visited, it was quite tense as the North tested recently inaugurated President Trump by launching ballistic missiles over Japan and flying drones across the DMZ. The colonel was very open with his briefing. His two high-school-aged children also attended so that they could appreciate the sacrifices made by soldiers not much older than them some sixty-seven years earlier on that same ground. Sandy stood in the blue building containing the conference table where the armistice was signed, flanked by South Korean guards on the North Korean side of the table.

Authur at P'anmunjŏm

We saw historic Taesŏng-tong village on the south side of the DMZ and the impressive but deserted Kijŏng-dong city on the north side. Also called Propaganda City, Kijŏng-dong consists of brightly painted multistory buildings and low-rise apartments lit brilliantly by electricity. Large loudspeakers blare Korean music and propaganda south continuously to entice defectors. A 525-foot flagpole proudly waves a 600-pound NK flag continuously, supposedly the largest flying flag in the world. We didn't see anyone within the city when we viewed it with binoculars from across the Freedom Bridge. We did hear the blaring music.

We visited the historic Changdeokgung Palace and the Korean Folk Village. Both illustrate the rich history and culture that the Koreans have developed over two thousand years. Korean *hanji* (paper) made from mulberry bark has been used for windows and doors for centuries. It is known to outlast other types of paper, including papyrus. The Korean written alphabet was invented in 1443 by King Sejong the Great and is called *Hangul*. It consists of twenty-eight letters and was created by the king to teach the common person how to be literate in the Korean language to replace the Chinese characters previously used. The Koreans are descendants of the Mongolian people and not the Chinese. Korean folklore, dress, and daily life are vividly brought to life at both locations.

We did get an afternoon of shopping in the Insa-dong neighborhood of Seoul. While there, an older Korean man kept following me around and saying something in Korean. I am sorry to admit that I was embarrassed and did not know what to do. I learned later that he was thanking my relatives for helping during the war. Everywhere we went in Korea, the locals knew who we were and why we were there. Of course, the large banners on the sides of our busses might have given them a hint of our identities. They were always grateful.

The food in Korea was delicious and sometimes adventurous. Many of our meals were at the hotel, which supplied a fantastic smorgasbord of traditional Korean and American dishes, both already prepared items and others made while you wait. We did stop at a couple of restaurants and a Korean BBQ for lunch while traveling to visit sites away from the hotel. Our favorite Korean dishes include bulgogi, bibimbap, and many types of kimchi. Though we never tried traditional *bosintang* (dog soup) while visiting, we did buy Korean red ginseng to improve stamina.

Our final evening in Korea included a formal dinner party with government and military dignitaries, including numerous politicians and the four-star general in charge of UN forces deployed in Korea. We were seated at a mixed table of American and Korean bigwigs, plus two well-behaved Korean youths in their equivalent of ROTC (Reserve Officers' Training Corps). The meal was traditional Korean and most excellent. Dinner entertainment included a projected sand artist and a youth choir. Dignitaries and family representatives made speeches. The evening concluded with each family representative receiving a Korean Ambassador for Peace Medal. For more information on the 2017 MPVA Revisit Korea trip, please visit www. youtube.com.

EPILOGUE

The Forgotten War ended with the signing of an armistice
more than sixty-five years ago. Few remain living who participated
in this police action, and those who are, are in their upper eighties or
older. Even their descendants are now in their sixties. According to
the DPAA, there are still 7,603[56] unaccounted from this war. Fifty-five
caskets were provided by North Korea in August 2018, of which 41
have now been identified. DPAA is analyzing these remains and will
first confirm that each belongs to a single individual before trying to
identify them. It may take years.

DPAA is the lead negotiation group with the North Koreans on
repatriating remains and hopes to gain access to conduct additional
searches. For the first time in ten years, the DPAA budget was fully
funded in 2018 and an additional $20 million allotted for Korean
War identification. The Department of Defense has approved the
systematic disinterment of all 867 unknown remains in the Punchbowl
over the next five to seven years for identification in seven distinct
batches based on where the remains were found. DPAA identified
218 remains in fiscal year 2018 (73 from the Korean War) and has a
target to identify 200 per year from now on. On 22 March 2019, Cpl.
Herschel M. Riggs was positively identified from the remains in the
Punchbowl. His nephew Tony Jasso attended the 2017 MPVA Revisit
Korea trip with us. Of course, even if all the outstanding remains were
located, it would still be another thirty-five years to identify them at

---

56   Statistics according to the DPAA website as of 6 December 2019

the full rate of 200 per year. The surviving veterans and immediate family will be long gone by then.

President Donald Trump met with Premier Kim Jong-un, the third-generation dictator of the hermit kingdom of North Korea, in Singapore on 12 June 2018. This first ever face-to-face meeting between the leaders of the two factions was cordial, and North Korea stopped test launching ballistic missiles afterward. Follow-on meetings have occurred between Kim Jong-un and Moon Jae-in, the current president of South Korea. On 19 September 2018, an agreement was reached to reduce tensions at the DMZ by removing select guard posts and antipersonnel mines and scheduling joint recovery of additional remains in early 2019. A second conference between Trump and Kim, held starting 26 February 2019, ended abruptly with Trump walking out when Kim requested all sanctions be lifted for limited denuclearization. Kim resumed missile testing 4 May 2019 by launching the new solid fuel KN-23 ballistic missile, which flies at a lower altitude and may maneuver in flight to confuse antimissile defenses. Technically, these tests did not breach the June 2018 Trump-Kim accord, and the US did not forcefully protest it. Only time will tell if these meetings will thaw relations between North and South long-term. Historically, meetings only work to the North's advantage with the South gaining little. Technically, the two countries are still at war.

Earlier in 2018, a doctoral candidate at Carnegie Mellon University contacted us for research for his thesis. Of mixed North Korean and Chinese descent, he is studying Korean War MIA and POW issues from a very different viewpoint. His dissertation examines the recovery, repatriation, and identification of the remains of American soldiers; its effects on the government and the families; and the impact on US foreign policy. As a couple of years have now passed since Uncle Donnie was laid to rest, Sandy was a bit circumspect in responding to his request for information. She finally settled on the word *closure* to summarize how she felt. Proving beyond a doubt that Corporal Donald Matney had died on the battlefield and had not languished in a foreign POW prison helped her and her Uncle Leonard and Aunt Ruth feel closure. No longer would they fear that he was lost or a coward or a prisoner locked in some unknown location.

But not all the families of the Korean War MIA/POWs have been so lucky. At least 69 American POWs were known to be alive at the end of the war and were never repatriated. The US government list of 944 that may have been alive and still held by the communists has never been resolved. John Zimmerlee thinks that the actual number retained alive after the armistice may be over 2,000. Only a few have ever been seen or heard from since. Maybe academic research can help pressure these former enemies to provide information on the missing held after the war.

The communists hoped that the indoctrination and brain washing of POWs who returned from Korea would provide them with future influence. But the virtues of a free society soon erased any "progressive" attitudes assumed during captivity. No Manchurian candidate or communist uprising resulted from their efforts to brainwash POWs returning to America or elsewhere. Seeing that the practice of indoctrination and "reeducation" was not worth the effort, POWs during the Vietnam War did not often experience it.

The North Korean regime even today holds the head of state supreme in a godlike status and treats the individual as interchangeable and expendable. They have proven this time again through their starvation of the masses so that the few can maintain power. Russia and Red China also followed this axiom, though both have become capitalistic in their economic approach lately. In socialistic society, all (except the elite) are "equal" with the individual holding no rights, only an obligation to serve the state. Life is still cheap at the individual level in North Korea. This was illustrated vividly in February 2017 when Premier Kim Jong-Un had his half brother Kim Jong-Nam openly assassinated at a Malaysian airport using a chemical weapon—a binary nerve agent.

Though Western philosophies are far from perfect, the individual is valued. Even during the harsh beginnings of the Korean War, when young draftees were sent into battle with minimal training and questionable armaments, they were respected and well-fed. When wounded, they were provided the best medical care possible. When killed, their remains were treated with respect and returned home. Even when missing, efforts are taken sixty-five years later to identify them and bury them per their relatives' wishes. In a democratic society, the individual has rights and opportunities, and the state has an obligation to serve the individual.

Today, refugees still flee from North Korea. Due to the DMZ, most travel by an underground railroad across the Tumen River into

China, then to Laos and Thailand, and finally into South Korea. Most are women and are vulnerable to deceit, abuse, and sex trafficking. All are welcomed by the ROK, and they are considered citizens according to constitutional law. However, adjusting to freedom can be hard. Unemployment for refugees is three times higher than average, over half suffer from depression, and about a third have thoughts about leaving the ROK because they don't fit in and miss their families and the structured life in the North.

Was the Korean War worth it? I can personally tell you that South Koreans will emphatically say, "Yes!" South Korea is one of the few nations on earth that transformed itself from a downtrodden third-world country into one of the most prosperous nations on earth, all due to the successful conclusion of the Korean War. South Korea today is economically strong and viable. Companies like Samsung, Hyundai, and LG are industry leaders throughout the world. Fifty-one million people call it home with 83 percent living in urban areas. Unlike the North that is barren and dark at night when seen from outer space, the South is bright, green, lush, and full of life. It boasts of one of the longest life expectancies and highest literacy rates of any country. It also has the fastest internet in the world.

Stalin and Kim felt that they could "liberate" South Korea within three weeks and that the US would never intervene. MacArthur proved them wrong. The war cost five million people their lives. The US spent $30 billion directly on fighting the war and much more on rebuilding South Korea afterward. Stalin learned that the US would fight a limited war, which the USSR exploited a few years later in Vietnam. The Kim dynasty retained power and think themselves world leaders still to this day. Religion other than Juche, which promotes the cult of the leader, is banned in the North. The South is religious tolerant. Latest estimates[57] measure South Korean religious beliefs as Korean Buddhism, 22.8%; Protestant Christianity, 18.3%; traditional shamanistic beliefs, 14.7%; new folk shamanistic beliefs, 14.2%; Korean Confucianism, 10.9%; Catholic Christianity, 10.9%; atheism or unaffiliated, 6.7%; and all others at 1.5%.

★ ★ ★

---

57   Sousa, Gregory, "Religious Beliefs in South Korea," World Atlas, 25 April 2017.

Three young men drove to the small train station in a tiny town in the heart of Missouri one hot August day in 1949. Two boarded a train for the army to discover the world. For six months, they both lived the good life performing occupational duty in Japan. Then suddenly, these two boated to Korea and were thrust into a violent police action that was really an intense war. Both died in battle a few weeks after leaving the security and tranquility of Japan. One came home and was buried immediately, and one came home sixty-six years later. Two were buried on the same day in the same cemetery back in their hometown. Only in America could this happen.

SO HOW DO I LOCATE MY LONG-LOST RELATIVE?[58]

When Sandy and I started our journey to locate Uncle Donnie, we had no idea what to do. We just attended the annual Defense POW/MIA Accounting Agency briefing and started to search. But you can learn from our experiences and from all others who have preceded you. If you have a loved one who disappeared in Korea or during the Cold War or during any other military event, here is an approach to help you learn more about what happened and may help locate their remains.

First, gather all the information available on your loved one—pictures, dental records, details on prior injuries (like traffic accidents or sports injuries), service ID (identification number), social security number, and fingerprints (if they were ever arrested). Physical characteristics are also important—estimated height, weight, age at time of disappearance, known tattoos, facial structure, and race. Any known friends or associates in the service may also be helpful.

Next, call the casualty office associated with your loved one's service: army—800-892-2490; air force— 800-531-5501;

---

58 Adapted from "Guide to Getting Answers" by John Zimmerlee at coalitionoffamilies.org.

marines—800-847-1597; and navy—800-443-9298. Provide your loved one's name and service ID number.[59] Ask if any other family members have been in contact. Ask who is listed as the primary next of kin. You can contact the official next of kin later to see if they have additional information. Request your loved one's IDPF file and any information that is available. Ask for the full field search case or full air loss case report. Request the unit's daily reports beginning at least two days before their loss date and ending at least two weeks later. Request a report of all the missing from the same incident for at least a couple of days each side of when he was reported missing.

Then offer to provide the case officer all the information that you have gathered. This will help them fill in any missing information. Remember that the case officer will have a number of open cases and that it will take time to gather the information, make copies, and send them to you—two to three months is not unusual.

The actual day your loved one disappeared is often the day before the reported date as the missing date is recorded when they don't show up for roll call. If the battle lasted more than one day, it is possible your loved one actually disappeared a day or two earlier. Once you receive the information from your case officer, determine who on the incident missing report returned home and who was captured. Then request the debriefing reports for all of them if they exist. Often debriefing reports will mention other names that are missed and not correlated otherwise. There are cases where a debriefing clearly states that someone was killed or captured, but this is never incorporated into the official reports.

There are a number of organizations who may be able to help. Members of the Coalition of Families (www.coalitionoffamilies. org), including John Zimmerlee, have extensive databases on missing and POWs from Korea and will exchange information if requested. The Korea War Project (www.koreanwar.org) maintains extensive databases, maps, DNA information, and references for veterans, families, researchers, and students. The POW Investigative Project (www.powinvestigativeproject.org) investigates reports of Americans

---

59   You can usually locate your loved one's service ID by searching for their name on government MIA or KIA lists such as at archives.gov.

secretly imprisoned by communist forces from the Korean, Cold, and Vietnam Wars. KPOWs (www.KPOWs.com) is dedicated to American prisoners kept in communist hands following the Korean War. The National Alliance of Families (www.nationalalliance.org) is dedicated to unearthing the truth on MIAs and prisoners held after the wars. And finally, the official Defense POW/MIA Accounting Agency (www.dpaa.mil) is the government agency charged with retrieving and identifying MIAs. All these organizations have resources that may help you in your search.

Finally, don't give up! It took us six years to make any progress. Stay in touch with others who are looking for their loved ones. Keep searching. Answers are out there.

LIST OF PRINCIPAL CHARACTERS

Charles "Brad" Smith (7 May 1916–23 May 2004). He was a colonel in the Twenty-First Infantry who led Task Force Smith at Osan on the first US battle against NKPA. He also commanded D Company, Thirty-Fifth Infantry, the first infantry to fight Japan in WWII in Hawaii.

Charles "Chuck" E. Farr (8 February 1930–24 February 1950). He was a corporal of the Sixteenth Reconnaissance First Cavalry. Chuck was the friend of Donald Matney from Seymour who took the train with him to basic training in 1949.

Donald "Donnie" Eugene Matney (11 April 1932–20 July 1950). He was a corporal in the US Army born in Seymour, Missouri, to Willa Tarbutton and Silas Matney in Matney Hollow. He died at the Battle of Taejon.

Douglas MacArthur (26 January 1880–5 April 1964). A five-star general Pacific commander, he received many awards, including the Medal of Honor. He also designed land-for-time strategy and the Inchon landing. He was sacked by Truman.

Guy S. Meloy Jr. (4 September 1903–14 December 1964). He was a colonel in command of the Nineteenth Infantry. He was wounded at

Kum River. He was promoted to four-star general in charge of Korea in the late 1950s.

Harry S. Truman (8 May 1884–26 December 1972). He was the president of US during the Korean War and was the one who fired MacArthur. He dropped the atom bomb on Japan to end WWII.

Joseph E. Peters (8 July 1933–15 November 2016). He was the younger friend of Donnie Matney who drove him to the train and was buried the same day as him at the same funeral home in Seymour, Missouri.

Joseph Stalin (18 December 1878–5 March 1953). He was the premier of the Soviet Union who guided Kim Il-Sung to attack South Korea. Under Stalin, the USSR provided arms and personnel and interrogated POWs.

Joseph S. Szito (2 June 1918–17 February 1993). He was a sergeant first class in charge of H Company mortars in the Nineteenth Infantry. He was field promoted to lieutenant and left the army as a staff sergeant. He was outspoken about the war.

Kim Il-Sung (15 April 1912–8 July 1994). He was the first supreme leader of North Korea. He fought in WWII with the Russians. His oldest son, Kim Jong-il, assumed premiership upon his death. He has a near-deity status in NK.

Mao Zedong (26 December 1893–9 September 1976). Chairman Mao was the founding father of Communist China. He directed the Chinese intervention into the Korean War and pushed for an armistice when Stalin died.

Paik Sun-yup (23 November1920–) He was a colonel, then general in charge of ROK First Division. He became the first ROK four-star general.

Paul F. Reagan (3 January 1921–20 March 1979). He commanded H Company Nineteenth Infantry. He had problems early on but received a Silver Star on November 1950. He left the army as a major.

Syngman Rhee (26 March 1875–19 July 1965). He was the first president of South Korea and a rebel against Russians and Japanese in the early 1900s. He fled to the US until after WWII. He was the president of the ROK until 1960. He was also exiled to Hawaii.

Walton H. Walker (3 December 1889–23 December 1950). He was a four-star general commander of the Eighth Army and coordinated the development of the Pusan Perimeter. He died in a freak jeep accident.

William F. Dean (1 August 1899–24 August 1981). He was major general of Nineteenth Infantry and was captured after the Battle of Taejon by NKPA. He received the Medal of Honor. He personally destroyed two T-34 tanks.

Woo Kyu-Chul (1932–). He is a fictional character, but his family name is from Taesŏng-tong. He is a refugee and sergeant of the ROK First Division, is married to Nabi, and has two children—daughter Sa-rang and son Seung. Aunt Sandara and Pak Him-chan are also fictional.

BIBLIOGRAPHY

24th Forward - The Pictorial History of the Victory Division in Korea	Sgt. Saul A. Stadtmauer, 1953
Twenty-Fourth Infantry Division Association's *Taro Leaf*	Volume 67, Issue 2, Spring 2013
Twenty-Fourth Infantry Division official journals	Declassified 9 December 2009
A Brief History of the 24th Infantry Division in Korea	1LT Shelby P Warren, editor, 2nd ed, September 1956
American Trophies: How US POWs Were Surrendered to North Korea, China, and Russia by Washington's "Cynical Attitude"	Mark Sauter, John Zimmerlee, 2013
Combat Actions in Korea	Russell A. Gugeler, 1987
"DMZ Not All That Peaceful for S. Korea Village"	Donald Smith, *National Geographic*, 28 August 1994
Fighting Jets	Bruce Walker, Time-Life Books, 1983

Fighting on the Brink: Defense of the Pusan Perimeter   Uzal W. Ent, 1996

H Company, Nineteenth Infantry Regiment, Morning Reports   Released 12 March 2012

Korean War Atrocities, US Senate Hearings   Eighty-Third Congress, January 11, 1954

Korean War Odyssey a.k.a. World War Three   R. L. Weiler, June 2000

MacArthur's Korean War Generals   Stephen R. Taaffe, 2016

Outstanding Leadership and Brilliant Victory   Pyongyng, DPRK, 1993

Sacrificial Lambs   Raymond C. Colton Sr., 2003

South to the Naktong, North to the Yalu   Roy E. Appleman, 2nd ed., 1992

Task Force Smith and the 24th Infantry Division in Korea   Maj. Raymond M. Longabaugh, 22 May 2014

The Dead, the Missing, and the Captured; Nineteenth Infantry   Joe Sweeney, 1998

The Hidden History of the Korean War, 1950–1951   I. F. Stone, 1952, reprinted 2014

The Korean War: The West Confronts Communism   Michael Hickey, 2001

The Organization Day Yearbook of the Nineteenth United States Infantry Regiment, 20 September 1949

When My Name Was Keoko   Linda Sue Park, 2002

INDEX OF PRINCIPAL PERSONS AND PLACES